# COUNSELING OLDER PERSONS
## *Careers, Retirement, Dying*

New Vistas in Counseling Series
*Series Editors*—Garry Walz and Libby Benjamin
*In collaboration with ERIC Counseling and Personnel Services Information Center*

**Structured Groups for Facilitating Development: Acquiring Life Skills, Resolving Life Themes, and Making Life Transitions, Volume 1**
Drum, D. J., Ph.D. and Knott, J. E., Ph.D.

**New Methods for Delivering Human Services, Volume 2**
Jones, G. B., Ph.D., Dayton, C., Ph.D. and Gelatt, H. B., Ph.D.

**Systems Change Strategies in Educational Settings, Volume 3**
Arends, R. I., Ph.D. and Arends, J. H., Ph.D.

**Counseling Older Persons: Careers, Retirement, Dying, Volume 4**
Sinick, D., Ph.D.

**Parent Education and Elementary Counseling, Volume 5**
Lamb, J. and Lamb, W., Ph.D.

**Counseling in Correctional Environments, Volume 6**
Bennett, L. A., Ph.D., Rosenbaum, T. S., Ph.D. and McCullough, W. R., Ph.D.

**Transcultural Counseling: Needs, Programs and Techniques, Volume 7**
Walz, G., Ph.D., Benjamin, L., Ph.D., et al.

**Career Resource Centers, Volume 8**
Meerbach, J., Ph.D.

**Behavior Modification Handbook for Helping Professionals, Volume 9**
Mehrabian, A., Ph.D.

# COUNSELING OLDER PERSONS
## *Careers, Retirement, Dying*

### DANIEL SINICK, PH.D.

*George Washington University*

*Vol. 4 in collaboration with ERIC Counseling
and Personnel Services Information Center New Vistas
in Counseling Series*
*Series Editors*—Garry Walz and Libby Benjamin

**HUMAN SCIENCES PRESS**
72 Fifth Avenue    3 Henrietta Street
NEW YORK, NY 10011 ● LONDON, WC2E 8LU

Library of Congress Catalog Number 77-21963
ISBN: 0-87705-312-X

Copyright © 1977 Human Sciences Press
72 Fifth Avenue, New York, N.Y. 10011

Printed in the United States of America
89 98765432

**Library of Congress Cataloging in Publication Data**

Sinick, Daniel.
    Counseling older persons.

    (New vistas in counseling; v. 4)
    Bibliography: p.
    1. Aged—Psychology. 2. Age and employment. 3. Retirement. 4. Death—Psychological aspects. 5. Counseling. I. Title. II. Series.
BF724.8.S5    362.6'042    77-21963    ISBN 0-87705-312-X

# CONTENTS

*Foreword*                                                          7

1. **Why Counselor Concern: An Overview**                           9
2. **Career Counseling**                                           17
   *Special Considerations with Older Clients*                     19
   *Counseling Emphases with Older Clients*                        24
3. **Retirement Counseling**                                       37
   *Special Considerations*                                        39
   *Counseling Emphases*                                           45
4. **Dying and Death**                                             55
   *Dying from Terminal Illness*                                   58
   *Taking One's Own Life*                                         65
   *Bereavement*                                                   72
5. **Trends, Issues, and Recommendations**                         79
   *Trends*                                                        81
   *Issues*                                                        85
   *Recommendations*                                               89

6. ***Appendices***                                                95
7. ***References***                                               105

# FOREWORD

The increasing percentage of older persons in the population has led to a greater awareness of their counseling needs. As people inevitably age and enter the closing phases of life, counseling can provide a much needed service in helping them choose second careers, plan for retirement, and prepare for death.

Aging and dying are events that all people must cope with in their own lives and in the lives of persons dear to them. While aging and dying are universal events, however, appropriate counseling responses have only recently developed. A basic resource that is useful to both the counseling generalist as well as the counselor who specializes in helping the aging and/or dying is long overdue. Dr. Sinick, we believe, has made a notable contribution by conceptualizing aging and its escalation at certain time periods as part of a lifelong dimension. This monograph communicates well the necessity of being knowledgeable about concerns accompanying the aging and dying processes for all counselors, whatever their predominant clientele.

It is in the tradition of the ERIC Counseling and Personnel Services Information Center to prioritize the development of publications which synthesize and bring together in one volume ideas, approaches, and resources on the cutting edge of new trends or developments. We believe that the Sinick monograph continues this tradition and offers a valuable resource to the reader, whether he/she be a professional helper, a paraprofessional, or one who is personally experiencing the difficulties of aging or the trauma of dying. Hopefully, it will stimulate the reader to delve further into the literature and to examine the burgeoning quantity of resources on this vital subject contained within the ERIC collection.

Garry R. Walz and Libby Benjamin
Director and Associate Director, ERIC/CAPS

*Chapter 1*

# Why Counselor Concern: An Overview

This introductory material highlights the need for counseling with older persons, the broad range of pertinent helping personnel, and the nature of counseling perspective and expertise required.

The increasing proportion of older persons in the population calls for increased attention to their counseling needs. As people approach the inevitable passages of aging and dying, they reach points where counseling can help them cope realistically and comfortably with these phases of life. Older persons continue to confront developmental tasks such as choosing second careers, planning for retirement, and dealing with death.

Counselors must concern themselves with the problems of aging and dying, not only from a personal standpoint, but because their clients—both young and old—experience the impact of these events.

While "events" is an appropriate word to apply to aging and dying in that they happen or occur, the term *process* more dynamically suggests how time is entailed in these stages. We all begin the process of aging and dying from the moment of conception (the Chinese count their birthdays from the date of conception). Within this lifelong process, however, there are shorter periods during which aging or dying escalates, whether physiologically of psychologically.

Counselors encounter clients who are either themselves going through various periods of aging or dying, whether they are actual or perceived, or whose lives are affected by others going through such periods. Aging and dying are thus pervasive processes that can take up an important part of counseling.

"Counseling" as used in this monograph is a generic term which involves a broad range of helping personnel, both professionals and paraprofessionals. Which practitioners would be most helpful in particular situations depends upon such variables as the clientele, the counseling focus, the setting, staffing patterns, and pertinent expertise. The aims of this monograph are to enhance expertise and widen the perspective of counseling.

## Pertinence to Counseling with Younger Persons

Aging and dying may enter into the counseling needs of younger persons in a number of ways. Young clients can improve their life plans by including lifespan concepts. By recognizing that youth and age are on a continuum, that "we" eventually become "they," the young can anticipate the effect of getting older on their personal, social, and vocational development.

Planful counseling over the lifespan does not require morbid preoccupation with physical debilitation and mental decrepitude. It does require considering possible career shifts, for example, and the need to be flexible in planning. Young women preparing for marriage and career(s) is a partial model of the lifespan approach.

This approach also properly takes into account planning for retirement from one or more careers. Young persons far from retirement can start to acquire interests and skills that might enrich their later years. Intrinsic to proper preparation for later life is an attitudinal expectation that avoids the all too common abruptness of aging and retirement.

Another way that aging becomes part of counseling younger persons is through their interaction with older persons. With their age differences counselors exert variable influences on their clients, as do parents, other relatives, and numerous older persons outside the family. People at various stages of aging may influence youngsters' personal development and vocational planning. Counseling may also concern the relationships shared between younger and older persons.

Finally, dying and death are confronted by young

persons as well as by older persons. They themselves, or persons important to them, may develop terminal medical conditions. They or others close to them may engage in self-destructive behavior, consciously or unconsciously. They may experience the loss of a loved one and a sense of bereavement. As a result, dying and its consequences can constitute part of the content of counseling younger clients.

## Older Persons May Require Counseling

What younger persons anticipate become actualities for older persons. They may have to abandon initial careers, whether voluntarily or involuntarily, in favor of second and sometimes third careers. Mature women enter or reenter the labor market. Retirement comes rushing in on the express track. Those idly awaiting events on the local track can benefit from the pacing and planning provided by counseling.

Interaction with younger persons is the other side of the coin already mentioned with respect to aging and counseling. Children and other younger persons are commonly regarded as on "the other side," too, of a generation gap. Whether this dichotomy is real or artificial, it often has to be dealt with in counseling. Stereotypes in the eyes of young and old beholders can be mitigated through counseling.

Younger persons are not the only ones with negative views of older people. Prejudices against aging persons are as plentiful as those against other "minority groups." The familiar terms *racism* and *sexism* have their parallel in *agism*. Consider the employment discrimination against older job applicants and how retirement is forced upon older, competent jobholders.

Agism infects older persons themselves and their closest relatives. The complaint of retirees' wives that their husbands "get under their feet" is no old wives' tale, nor is it funny. Older persons are caught up in the controversy raised over continuing to participate in life's activities versus "disengagement" and "growing old gracefully." The latter alternative, some think, makes litter of the living, with the subliminal blessing of "good riddance to bad rubbish."

Considering dying and death enters into counseling with older persons, even more so than with younger persons. Terminal medical conditions, self-destructive behavior, and bereavement are experienced with increasing frequency as one's age increases. As with the other problems of older persons, these can be alleviated by the compassion and expertise of counselors.

### Focus of This Monograph

This overview of aging and dying as they relate to counseling has included younger as well as older clients as prospects for pertinent assistance. If younger persons become sensitive and oriented to the developments of later life and include these aspects in their planning, they will be better prepared for what otherwise can be threatening, even devastating, life stages. Counselors similarly oriented and sensitized can render a sorely needed service.

The focus of this particular monograph is on the perspective and expertise counselors need to serve older persons in regard to aging and dying. Implications for earlier counseling touching these topics will be abundant, whether direct or indirect. The focus spotlights three areas of counseling with older clients: (1) counseling regarding careers; (2) counseling regarding retirement; (3) and counseling regarding dying and death.

## SUMMARY

This introductory chapter indicates that counselors and other helping personnel—both professionals and para-professionals—have a role to play with respect to the developmental tasks of older persons who change careers, reach retirement, and confront dying and death. Since older persons can benefit from counseling, practitioners must be equipped with the proper perspective and expertise.

*Chapter 2*

# CAREER COUNSELING

As older persons change careers, or enter and reenter the labor force, they can be helped to evaluate their motivations and characteristics toward finding self-actualizing occupational roles.

## SPECIAL CONSIDERATIONS WITH OLDER CLIENTS

Career counseling with older clients needs to take into account a number of special considerations. Since career changes among clients are common, consideration must be given the reasons behind them. General characteristics of older clients need attention and comprehension; individual clients are more likely to differ in degree than in kind. Although there is legislation to prevent age discrimination, employer practices with regard to (and often without respect to) older workers must be considered.

### Why People Change Careers

Underlying the numerous individual decisions to make career changes are broad sociological, technological, and economic developments. The longer lifespan alone permits one to pursue more than one career within one's life. Among the trends that tend to push people toward second and third careers are retirement at earlier ages, earlier completion of families, disruption of families by divorce as well as by death, the feminist movement, and the polarization of sociopolitical views (mainly materialism versus humanism). In business and industry workers are replaced by automated machines while company mergers and acquisitions put others out of work. New occupational specialities and opportunities emerge. Paid work is accorded higher value than volunteer activities. Women switch from homemaking to breadwinning, assisted by increased child care services. Affluence of individuals or families affords the wherewithal for career changes. Funds available to veterans, widows, and others may also make preparation for career changes possible (Sheppard, Ullmann, Cooperman, & Samler, 1971).

On top of the broad trends are more personal pushes and pulls that move people out of one career and into another. Counselors and clients need to recognize and distinguish avoidance motivations and approach motivations, desires to get out versus drives to get in. Similarly, rational versus emotional bases for career changes must be distinguished. Any of the accompanying "Reasons People Change Careers" could be rationales or rationalizations.

*Reasons People Change Careers*

Initial career not person's own choice
Career inappropriate from outset
Original aspirations not met by career
Purpose of first career accomplished
Change of career required by changing goals
Satisfaction sought for higher-level needs
Dead end reached in terms of advancement
Inadequate outlet for creativity
Insufficient challenge to abilities
Data-People-Things involvement inappropriate
Incongruence with vocational interests
Desire to implement avocational interests
Disproportion between prescribed and discretionary duties
Insufficient variety in work content
Work pressures and deadlines too demanding
Work becoming too physically demanding
Work context source of dissatisfactions
Employer policies and practices dissatisfying
Purpose of employer enterprise incompatible

Co-workers divergent in values and lifestyles
Personality conflicts with supervisor or co-workers
Earnings outstripped by living expenses
Desire to "keep up with the Joneses"
Social status of occupation inadequate
Insufficient time for leisure activities
Greener grass in another field

While all the reasons do not apply to all clients, those which are applicable need to be sorted out and analyzed. In addition to their avoidance-approach and rational-emotional elements, the duration or persistence of each reason demands consideration. What efforts have been made to modify longstanding situations? Have short-term dissatisfactions been given a chance to change? Is enough known about parallel factors in prospective careers?

Careful consideration of individual dynamics involved in the reasoning, thoughtful weighing (qualitative only) of salient variables, and application of pertinent information may enable client and counselor to come up with a wise decision. Career change is appropriate for some clients, but not for others. Someone once said, "When it is not necessary to change, it is necessary not to change."

### Characteristics of Older Clients

"Older" is purposely not defined in this monograph because it is obviously a relative term that varies from individual to individual at a rate that is too great for chronological age to serve as an adequate index. Different people mature at different developmental tempos. They grow up and grow old in response to different combinations of genetic and environmental inputs. Physiological and psychological characteristics may be as diverse within age groups as between age groups.

Sociological forces, on the other hand, are so largely functions of time periods that they confer different characteristics on different generations. Those reared within a particular time period have experienced the history, culture, economics, and educational qualities and opportunities of that period. Counselors must try to understand each individual as a figure against the ground of his or her generation.

Yet, several characteristics of people seeking second careers may complicate counseling. Many persons are found to lack self-confidence, the skills required for their career choice, and the skills required in jobseeking. Counselors need to understand these common inadequacies and know how to deal with them.

Such shortcomings are often those of women whose first career was interrupted by child-rearing or whose only career was that of a housewife. Entering or reentering the labor force with few skills or rusty ones can generate fear of failure and related anxieties. Career women may have anxieties arising from unequal pay, other inequities, and the struggle for parity. Although space does not permit separate treatment of women in this monograph, Appendix 1 provides a list of "Readings Related to Older Women" for the convenience of interested readers.

Lack of self-confidence, perhaps paradoxical in persons making a career change, frequently seems to be based on false ideas and perceptions. Older clients may apply agist generalizations to themselves, sometimes out of a sense of being "realistic." Affirming, "Let's face it," they may see themselves as slower physically or mentally, shorter of memory, less capable and adaptable. They start believing, "You can't teach an old dog new tricks." They may fail to perceive the importance of personal qualities such as reliability, resourcefulness, stability, and sensitivity.

Lack of the skills required in choosing careers and

seeking jobs is generally the result of lack of practice in these activities. First careers are often entered with little or no deliberate process of choice, and jobhunting is commonly a haphazard course. Career choice is hampered, too, by overconcern with "irreversibility," clinging to distinctions between "men's jobs" and "women's jobs," and unfamiliarity with the transferability of work skills. Counselors can familiarize clients with transferability concepts, the increasing opening of occupations to either sex, and Ginzberg's (1972) reversal of irreversibility.

*Pertinent Employer Practices*

Even older clients equipped with excellent jobseeking skills may still have to contend with the practices and prejudices of employers. If agism infects older persons themselves and friends and relatives sympathetic with them, it is a veritable epidemic among employers impersonally oriented toward making profits. Although profit-making motivations are valid in our society, myopic monetary considerations can blur humanitarian concern.

Employers can balance both concerns when they realize that it is often to their own advantage. Bringing about such realization is discussed later in this chapter. Employers unaware of the advantages of employing older workers operate on the basis of arbitrary hiring requirements and biased personnel procedures.

Despite legislation against use of age as a criterion in hiring, the record of job placement of older persons indicates only erratic observance of the laws. Frequently standard procedures used to screen job applicants are manipulated as artificial barriers that prevent hiring people who could actually function effectively on the job. These procedures include pre-employment medical exams, tests standardized on younger persons, and even routine job interviews.

## COUNSELING EMPHASES WITH OLDER CLIENTS

Some emphases for counselors have already been implied or indicated in relation to bases for career change, pertinent client characteristics, and obstructive practices of employers. Counselors who are aware of the complexity of reasons for seeking different careers can deal in appropriate depth with the dynamics involved. Complicating characteristics of clients can similarly be incorporated with sensitivity in counseling. Counseling practices must also respond to and anticipate employer practices. Needed emphases now require further explication.

### Evaluating Motivations and Goals

Even older clients do not necessarily know where they are "coming from" or where they want to go. Basic trust between client and counselor does not mean that the counselor should believe everything the client says. To do so might result in ill-considered planning based on misperceived motivations, blurred goals, and erroneous information. A client may unconsciously be implementing the motivations of relatives or significant others and in effect, his or her goals be those of others. Information regarding a past or future career may be biased or inaccurate.

One purpose of counseling is to help clients accurately perceive their motivations and goals, their potentialities and limitations, and information relevant to these and related variables. Evaluation is basically a process centering on the client's participation, the desired outcome being *self-evaluation*. While theoretical progress is represented by increased emphasis on client participation, the evaluation process is better viewed as one in which the counselor participates to assist the client.

Clients can be helped to review their verbalized reasons for changing careers and to become aware of less conscious reasons, when this will enable them to make a wiser career choice. Hidden motivations should not be uncovered to satisfy the curiosity of the counselor.

Straightforward situations occur frequently in counseling. Consider a successful pharmacist who chose that career to advance a low socio-economic level, and whose family is now financially, educationally, and emotionally secure. He wishes to switch to a career more compatible with basic values long deferred. His values pertain less to money-making than to achieving increased self-actualization by implementing previously untapped interests and abilities.

Some variations on this theme, as well as more devious themes, are based on self-deception that needs to be dealt with honestly by client and counselor together. The client's insistence that his or her abilities are unchallenged, creativity is stifled, and higher-level needs are unsatisfied turn out to be illusions shaped by a desperate desire to escape work pressures and deadlines. Finally recognizing the avoidance motivation is often the first step toward realistic planning for a career change.

*Generating Self-Confidence*

Lack of self-confidence in second career seekers is so common as to require special counseling attention. To develop self-confidence, both client and counselor must counteract devaluating misconceptions about the aging process as well as personal misperceptions of employment potentials. Toward both these troublesome areas, positive attitudes must be shaped.

Counselors can draw upon sound material that debunks mental decline in older persons and other depreciative notions (Green, 1972). Here are examples of pertinent information that can be introduced into second career counseling as needed (Grace, 1968, pp. 26–53):

- —From biological maturity until age 60, physical strength seems to be maintained at its maximum.
- —Maximum intellectual functioning appears to occur between the ages of 45 and 80.
- —Available evidence shows little change in the ability to learn new skills and acquire new information between ages 20 and 65.
- —Vocabulary, information, and comprehension tests show little, if any, decline with age through the 60's.
- —The functions of learning and memory, for the most part, are not significantly affected by aging.
- —The middle-aged or older worker may be able to transfer learning from earlier experiences to new situations.
- —Morale (one's feeling about his current work and future prospects) drops very low in the late 20's, but rises to new highs in the late 50's.
- —As a worker approaches later years, his motivation toward making a lasting impression on the firm, on the task, and on society in general increases.

What impresses some clients even more than these empirical findings are the favorable attributes of older workers mentioned by employers themselves. Self-confidence may be given a needed boost by this slightly adapted, significant list (U. S. Department of Labor, 1956, p. 8):

- —Stability
- —Steady work habits
- —Less waste of time

—Greater reliability
—Less absenteeism
—Responsibility and loyalty
—Serious attitude toward job
—Less supervision required
—Less distraction by outside interests
—Greater inclination to stay on job

Perceptions of personal inadequacies can frequently be counterbalanced through a joint effort to recall relatively successful experiences in life. Any achievements, from childhood on, that yielded favorable comments from parents, peers, or others can serve as a base on which to build self-confidence. Even a modicum of praise for any avocational or vocational activities the client pursued can sustain self-confidence and also suggest avenues for exploring a second career. For some clients such avenues may be suggested and their self-confidence lifted by vicariously experiencing the second career successes of others (Stetson, 1971).

*Minimizing Use of Tests*

There are two general reasons why the use of testing should be minimized for older clients. One reason is the inadequacy of the traditional testing approach with such clientele. The other is the availability of more effective approaches.

Most tests employed in counseling were aimed at younger persons with the intent to measure or predict performance in school. These tests place a premium on speed, visual acuity, and other variables that may be extraneous to what is being evaluated. Their norms are commonly inapplicable to older persons, who, in addition, may not have any recent experience in taking tests. Older clients are even more sensitive than younger ones to a test's apparent lack of any meaningful criterion. When lack of face validity is accompanied by lack of predictive validity, other types of technical validity have little practical utility.

Since test results are likely to be unfavorable, whether in whole or in part, self-confidence may be further impaired. On the other hand, a small proportion of older clients can profit a good deal from positive test results, provided their self-confidence does not rise disproportionately to their prospective careers. Good test results, like poor ones, may not be predictive of career performance.

Although inventories to tap interests and personality traits are free of time limits, they present most of the other shortcomings mentioned regarding tests of aptitude or achievement. Apart from the problems usually found in testing, such as forced choices, response styles, and faking—whether conscious or unconscious— inventories have their own flaws. Client motivations to do well or poorly on particular tests have their counterpart motivations for favorable or unfavorable facades as reflected by inventory profiles.

The artificiality of tests and inventories accounts for much of their inadequacy, especially with older clients. The emphasis in recent years on a naturalistic approach to both assessment and research is particularly relevant to clients with more extensive life histories (Dailey, 1971). Longitudinal data are likely to yield more realistic information about clients than cross-sectional data. Real-life experiences, including work experiences (Leshner & Snyderman, 1963), are natural sources of information regarding such matters as performance, perceptions, and preferences.

Whether or not questionnaires or autobiographies are used in eliciting information from clients' life histories and work histories, interviews are a substantial means of generating understanding and self-understanding of clients. Interviews go beyond interest inventories, for example, in tapping intensity of interest, duration of interest, and reasons underlying interest as they are more personal and flexible. The pertinence of such aspects of interest and personality assessment has given recognition to the importance of expressed interests and other dynamics accessible through interviews (Whitney, 1969).

*Putting Old Skills and Interests to Work*

An axiom of career counseling is to ascertain a client's assets and invest them in appropriate planning. Acquired abilities, unfolded interests, and matured personal traits make up a pattern from the past to be utilized in the future. It would be uneconomical and even wasteful not to draw further returns from earlier investments. While this financial metaphor can be applied successfully in counseling for second careers, counselor and client must do so with discrimination. Some career changes are so drastic as to limit the application of transferability concepts.

Transferability denotes a process that is built into the *Dictionary of Occupational Titles* (U. S. Department of Labor, 1965, 1966, 1968b) to facilitate comparisons of client characteristics and occupational characteristics. The traits included for possible comparisons are abilities or aptitudes, interests, temperaments, physical activities, environmental factors, general educational development, specific vocational preparation, and level of work complexity in relation to data, people, and things. Volume II of the DOT provides combinations of acquired skills and preferences, together with prior experiences, in school or out, that might be pertinent to particular kinds of work.

The military services employ transferability in the course of induction and, more relevant to this monograph, in the course of discharge. The DOT and related tools, used to convert civilian experience into military assignments, are used in reverse to utilize military experience for civilian occupations. *Target—Tomorrow: Second Career Planning for Military Retirees* (U. S. Department of Defense, 1970) has helpful content for nonmilitary clients as well, as does a book by Collings (1971).

Acquired attributes can be used as points of departure for exploring both formal and informal groups of occupations (Sinick, 1970). Formal classifications like that of the DOT are easily supplemented by informal groupings particularly related to client characteristics. For example, school subjects clients liked or in which they did well suggest possible related occupations that can be explored with the aid of various materials (Brochard, 1971; Malnig & Morrow, 1975; Steinberg, 1964; U. S. Department of Labor, 1967a), including a free series of brochures updated every two years (U. S. Department of Labor, even years).

*Developing New Skills and Interests*

When desires for drastic career changes indicate sharp departures from past experience, counseling may proceed accordingly. Whether there are new motivations or old motivations functioning autonomously, realizing the new goals may require setting aside acquired skills and interests in favor of new ones. The need for new skills and interests could be revealed through the emphases discussed earlier: evaluation of motivations and goals, generation of self-confidence, test and nontest tapping of attributes, and efforts to apply old attributes.

How are new skills and interests developed? Two major ways are education or training in school settings and job tryouts in work settings. Whichever approach is employed, careful thought needs to be given to whether it should be a full-time or part-time involvement. Exploring a new field and how one relates to it on a full-time basis has merit, but loss of income and continuity with abandonment of employment may require thoughtful consideration. In other words, it is sometimes safer not to venture forth until part-time exploration opens up a new avenue.

Clients differ in their educational level and in how much time they wish to devote to additional education or training. To help cope with these differences there are five inexpensive brochures (U. S. Department of Labor, 1968a) which use the terms "Jobs" interchangeably with "Occupations":

1. Jobs for which a high school education is generally required.
2. Jobs for which a high school education is preferred, but not essential.
3. Jobs for which junior college, technical institute, or other specialized training is usually required.
4. Jobs for which a college education is usually required.
5. Jobs for which apprenticeship training is available.

Whitfield and Hoover (1968) cite 145 occupations generally requiring no more than two years of training beyond high school. For clients able and willing to aim higher, Hiestand (1971) offers a scholarly study of career changes requiring professional preparation. He includes in-depth discussion of the dynamics involved in making such changes. "Continuing education," a highly relevant concept, is a term incorporated in the titles of directories pursuing the subject. These directories are guides to a variety of such programs for adults (Goodman, 1968; Thomson, 1972; U. S. Department of Labor, 1971b).

Education—or at least related credentials—can be achieved in some instances without formal class attendance. *Get credit for what you know* (U. S. Department of Labor, 1971c) provides information about such opportunities as the high school equivalency diploma and college level examinations for academic credit, as well as home study through correspondence and television programs. An external degree program is described (McGarraghy, 1973) in a special issue of *Industrial Gerontology* on second careers.

Job tryouts in work settings constitute the other general approach to or "the development of" developing new skills and interests. Whether or not such development can be accomplished by education affirmed by credits and credentials, it can be achieved through substantive education and actual work exploration. Since job tryouts are not easy to come by, however, they are treated along with other employment difficulties in the next section.

*Overcoming Employment Obstacles*

Although obtaining employment on a trial basis is sometimes easier than obtaining full-time employment, those seeking second careers—and their counselors—must anticipate obstacles in their path. Employers often have negative stereotypes about older persons, which have little or no basis in general and little or no applicability in particular. Paradoxically, employers may be older persons themselves whose work performance belies their beliefs.

The paradox is partly explained by the natural tendency to see *others* as older persons with inadequacies brought on by added years. Employers often justify their stereotypes and their reluctance to hire older workers with the excuse that they are in business to make profits and older workers are considered unprofitable investments. This explanation does not account for similar reluctance on the part of employers in the not-for-profit sector.

The stereotypes are actually rationalizations and have also been characterized as myths at odds with realities. From studies conducted by the U. S. Department of Labor and other agencies, the accompanying "Myths and Facts Regarding Older Workers" (somewhat condensed here) have been reported (U. S. Department of Labor, 1971a).

## MYTHS AND FACTS REGARDING OLDER WORKERS

| The Myth | The Fact |
|---|---|
| 1. Older workers are too slow—they can't meet the production requirements. | 1. Studies show no significant drop in performance and productivity. Many older workers exceed the average output of younger employees. |
| 2. Older workers can't meet the physical demands of jobs. | 2. Job analysis indicates that less than 14% of all jobs require great strength and heavy lifting. Labor-saving machinery enables older workers to handle most jobs without difficulty. |
| 3. You can't depend on older workers—they're absent from work too often. | 3. According to surveys, workers 65 and over have a good record of attendance in comparison with other age groups. |
| 4. Older workers are not adaptable—they're hard to train | 4. Evaluations of older jobseekers show that a high propor- |

because they can't accept change.

tion are flexible in accepting a change in their occupations and earnings. Actually, many young people are set in their ways, while many older workers adjust to change readily.

5. Hiring older workers increases pension and insurance costs.

5. Costs of group life, accident, and health insurance and workmen's compensation are not materially increased by hiring older workers. Small additional pension costs, when incurred, are more than offset by the older worker's experience, lower turnover, and quality of work.

The reluctance of employers can be reduced by alerting them to these "facts of life," as well as the other favorable attributes of older workers presented in the earlier section on "Generating Self-Confidence." This sound information regarding the positive potential of older workers, along with the favorable attributes of a particular client, prepares experienced job placement personnel to counter employer objections.

There are three specific ways that employers can be further assisted in the hiring of older persons. Concerning techniques in training new workers, Belbin (1968, 1970) delineated a "discovery method" whereby task-oriented difficulties encountered by older persons are accommodated by appropriate adaptations in training techniques. Koyl (1970, 1974) concentrated on the means of matching workers and jobs, and developed an assessment scale called GULHEMP that can be used to compare a person's profile of seven job relevant variables (general physique, upper extremities, lower extremities, hearing, eyesight, mentality, and personality) with the requirements of specific jobs. And redesigning jobs to fit workers (Griew, 1964; Marbach, 1968; U. S. Department of Labor, 1967b) has become an increasingly acceptable alternative or complement to the traditional fitting of workers to jobs.

## SUMMARY

Since older persons change careers for a variety of reasons, they must assess their motivations and goals together with their individual characteristics and employer practices before adopting a plan of action. Self-confidence may have to be generated, as old skills and interests are put to work or new ones developed. Procedures are suggested for accomplishing these ends and for overcoming obstacles to employment.

*Chapter 3*

# RETIREMENT COUNSELING

The developmental stage of counseling for retirement calls for further stock-taking, preparation for role adjustments, planning for optimal use of time, and managing matters such as income, housing, and health.

Retirement counseling requires separate treatment from career counseling because not all who retire go on to second careers. Other alternatives may include continued employment that does not necessarily constitute a career. This chapter focuses on other options and the planning needed to optimize them.

Retirement planning, retirement preparation, and retirement education are broad terms used to emphasize the need for a transition from the role of worker to that of retiree. The difference in the social status of these roles is part of the problem calling for preparation and planning. Pre-retirement is another term frequently used to put added emphasis on the value of thought and action prior to the date of retirement.

## SPECIAL CONSIDERATIONS

For clients retiring but seeking second careers, the special considerations and counseling emphasis presented in Chapter 2 would be pertinent. Much of the contents of Chapter 2 might also be applicable in discussing other options available in retirement. Retirement counseling must consider why prior planning is advisable, what attitudinal and role adjustments can be anticipated, what options for use of time may be available, and what additional areas of potential retirement difficulty require planning.

### Why Planning is Needed

With more people living longer and retirement often

arriving earlier, increasing numbers of older persons are abruptly confronted by changes they are not prepared for. Early retirement, whether voluntary or mandatory, curtails the time needed to take stock of one's situation and make appropriate plans. If the decision for early retirement is voluntary, it is vital that it be made with due deliberation, proper planning, and perhaps counseling.

Clients can be helped to appreciate the value of planning in various phases of life—sometimes by hindsight of situations where prior planning was lacking. It can be pointed out that planning is important to making such decisions as choosing an occupation, choosing a mate, and whether to rent or buy something. Applying this concept to retiring minimizes the possibility of trial-and-error approaches to this important juncture in life.

The desirability of planning for retirement can be supported by the findings of empirical studies. One such investigation (U. S. Civil Service Commission, 1968) found that nine out of ten retired or eligible for retirement employees were in favor of retirement planning programs and liked the programs they attended; over two-thirds considered the programs they attended useful. Another study (Draper, Lundgren, & Strother, 1967) reported that those who had made plans found higher retirement satisfaction.

Programs of planning or preparation for retirement generally put more emphasis on education rather than counseling. Their sessions are often a series of lectures where experts speak on retirement-oriented topics to large classes of pre-retirees. If no individual assistance is provided, such programs resemble group guidance in educational settings. While instructional programs that present pertinent information to interested groups are no doubt beneficial, individual and group counseling can help clients cope more effectively with personal attitudes, adjustments, and options.

## Attitudes and Role Adjustments

Out of the multitude of client attitudes that might affect retirement planning, adjustment, and satisfaction, several salient ones demand special consideration. In a culture that is enamored of youth, negative attitudes toward aging, such as agist prejudices mentioned earlier, are bound to exist. Young persons should be treated with dignity and respect, but so should older persons.

"The youth orientation of our society," points out Tiven (1971, p. 102), "discourages people from wanting to identify themselves as old." Max Lerner commented that "the most flattering thing one can say to an American is that he doesn't look his age, as if looking old were the most damning thing in the world." The fact that growing older is not damning everywhere in the world could be a source of added self-esteem for some clients.

The predominance of the work ethic in our society encourages negative attitudes toward retirement. Although slightly eroded in recent years, the Protestant ethic is still a rock of Poor Richard prudence and productivity on which are dashed the hopes of workers reaching retirement. As they feel unproductive and useless, many clients need to replace the concept of *retirement from* with that of *retirement to*. They need to adopt the philosophy of Charles Kettering: "My interest is in the future, because I am going to spend the rest of my life there."

An attitude corollary to the view of retirement as a cut-off to life is one that regards retirement as tantamount to death. Anxieties regarding dying and death are dealt with in Chapter 4, but they often enter into retirement counseling. They generate such defenses as blaming oneself for the presumably sad state of affairs, casting blame upon others, or demonstrating depression and dependence.

During retirement, role adjustments must be made in relation to the differential attitudes and defenses adopted by retirees and the differential treatments accorded them by others. Are benighted breadwinners regarded as no longer worth their salt? Do dignity and respect go down the drain? Is a person without work regarded as a person without wisdom? Is the one who was looked up to now looked down upon? "Role reversal in a family," comments Koller (1968, p. 139), "appears to be one of the most difficult changes older persons face. An 'independent' parent becomes a 'dependent' child, or a formerly 'dependent' child assumes the prerogatives of an 'independent' parent."

*Options for Use of Time*

The work ethic, together with other cultural constraints, has made working full-time the *sine qua non* of our society and anything less than that sinful. Many persons about to retire may therefore think of second careers as the only viable option. But just as man does not live by bread alone, men and women can find more to life during retirement than continued full-time employment for pay.

Part-time or temporary employment affords some continued income as well as other rewards of paid work. "Opportunities for part-time and part-year employment have grown substantially," reports a publication on older workers (U. S. Department of Labor, 1971d, p. 2). The projection is equally favorable: "Growth in part-time opportunities will likely parallel growth in workers who prefer part-time jobs" (U. S. Department of Labor, 1970, p. unnumbered). The burgeoning of employment agencies specializing in temporary jobs indicates an increase in opportunities for such work.

Unpaid volunteer work offers opportunities for use of one's free time on a full-time, part-time, or temporary basis. Both growth and diversity of such opportunities have been reported (U. S. Department of Labor, 1969, p. 1): "There are: (1) more volunteers, (2) different kinds of volunteers, (3) different kinds of functions, and (4) different channels for the delivery of their services."

Continuing education, mentioned in the Chapter 2 section on "Developing New Skills and Interests," is another constructive way of using one's free time. The proliferation of community colleges, which offer low-cost courses of great variety with or without credit, give older persons access to education. A perhaps serendipitous benefit of continuing education and its intellectual stimulation is that it possibly increases longevity (Palmore & Jeffers, 1971; Rose & Bell, 1971).

Avocational activities can be constructive and creative outlets for retirees, too. However, this is often more easily said than done. The work ethic has dimmed or distorted the view many people adopt toward nonwork activities. "Older people tend to equate industry with virtue," says Carp (1968, p. 15), "and they have had little acquaintance with leisure." Pastimes to kill free time can be supplemented or supplanted by self-actualizing activities.

*Other Retirement Difficulties*

In addition to all the matters already mentioned, retirement planning commonly takes into account such considerations as income and finances, housing and living arrangements, health and nutrition, consumer education and personal safety, and legal affairs. Ranging from mundane to major, these represent areas of vital concern—and of potential difficulty—during retirement.

Amount of income anticipated during retirement may affect attitudes, role adjustments, options available or desirable, housing, health, safety—any of the potential areas of difficulty. Sources of income must be considered, together with projected expenses as the future cost of living may require unaccustomed austerity, budgeting, and borrowing.

Where to live during retirement can be a major decision creating happiness or havoc. Should one stay in familiar territory with family and friends or set out for a sunswept *terra incognita*? Should one live together with relatives or separately, with other "senior citizens" or where age groups mix? Is public or private housing preferable?

There are preventive and remedial aspects of physical and emotional well-being that call for retirement planning. They include exercise and rest, the balancing and timing of food intake, symptom detection and use of medication, care of specific parts of the body, and Medicare vs. Medicaid.

Consumer education cuts across other areas that can improve the income-expense ratio. Such areas include knowledge of sound purchasing of products and services, housing conveniences, nutrition and health, vocational and avocational activities, and selection and use of a lawyer. Knowing how to distinguish between "Best Buys" and "Good-byes," cooperative apartments and condominiums, calories and carbohydrates, recreation expense and recklessness, and legal and illegal fees can extend both dollars and life.

Life itself may depend upon cautious concern with personal safety, without being paranoid about imminent peril. Caution prevents common household and outdoor accidents, and robbery at home or in the streets. How to cope, including legal redress, can be known in advance.

Older persons should be aware that they can rely on

the counsel of lawyers before and after numerous situations. If loans are incurred, contracts negotiated, houses sold or bought, other living arrangements made, marriages ended or started, businesses begun, or wills executed, a reputable attorney can help them to avoid or alleviate possible legal entanglements.

## COUNSELING EMPHASES

As with "Special Considerations," much of the Chapter 2 contents on emphases needed in career counseling with older clients might be applicable to retirement counseling. Motivations and goals might need to be evaluated, self-confidence generated, use of tests minimized, old skills and interests put to work, new ones developed, and employment obstacles overcome. Additional emphases in retirement counseling must be placed on accepting retirement as another positive phase of life, adjusting attitudes and roles, considering part-time work for pay, working as a volunteer, using free time creatively, and coping with other complexities of retirement.

### Facing Another Phase of Life

Emphasis on retirement as part of living is essential for effective planning and counseling with clients who view retirement as a phase of dying. Kathryn Close recognizes this in her book, *Getting Ready to Retire* (1972). She puts her finger on the various changes that make up the central problem of retirement, such as changes in status, occupation, income, living arrangements, and physical capacity. She goes on to point out that "they can be met with sound and imaginative planning that can make the period of retirement as meaningful a part of the span of life as any other" (p. 3).

Counselors as well as clients may have difficulty

accepting the concept that retirement is a natural period in normal life development. Since professional literature gives scant attention to the middle and later years, understanding of this period has been kept at a minimum. Textbooks on human development tend to focus on the early years, largely disregarding the developmental tasks of adulthood and advanced maturity. "Middlescence" and senescence have fared better, however, in some recent books (for example, Botwinick, 1973; Butler & Lewis, 1973; Eisdorfer & Lawton, 1973; Kimmel, 1974; Puner, 1974).

A further source of difficulty for counselors as well as clients is the prevalence of agist stereotypes and biases. Unfortunately, counselors are apparently not immune to agism (Schlossberg, Vontress, & Sinick, 1974), either by selection for programs of preparation or by professional preparation itself. Troll and Schlossberg (1971, p. 20) came to this conclusion: "On the basis of this study it seems evident that counselors of adults need to take a close look at themselves with regard to their own age bias." Filling the absence of understanding of aging with biases and stereotypes about age only hinders rather than helps clients confronting retirement.

## Adjusting Attitudes and Roles

Clients can be helped by counselors who are free—or at least aware—of biases, who appreciate the capabilities as well as the limitations of older persons, and who accept retirement as a worthy stage in life development. When counselors add their own negative attitudes to those of the client, needed adjustment is unlikely to occur. Peers with positive attitudes can sometimes be of greater assistance.

Recognizing that retirement is not quite death is often difficult to accomplish because of a sense of loss that complicates adjustment. At retirement, as in many situations in life, bitter-sweet feelings are entirely appropriate. Bitterness over what has been lost must give way, however, to pleasantness over what is yet to come. In the process, clients may have to go through a period very much like that of mourning the loss of a loved one or loss of a limb.

This parallel has been clarified by Smith, Kendall, and Hulin (1969, p. 133):

> The process of adjusting to retirement and getting to like it will take as long as is required for the person to alter his frame of reference and accept the new anchor points specified by the realities of his new situation, just as adjustment to the loss of a limb is dependent, in the first instance, on acceptance of the fact that the limb is gone.

The "phantom limb" phenomenon need not be compensated for by a fantasized perpetuation of youth. Adjustment to getting older does not require a client to reply to a counselor's inquiry, "Do you feel younger or older than your chronological age?," by exclaiming, "Much younger!" Clients who answer, "Younger," "Older," or "Neither," may be following personalized paths to their individual adjustments. Counselors familiar with the different paths can effectively serve as guides.

Related to these self-perceptions and the sense of loss is the retiree's handling of the issue of disengagement versus continued active participation in life. Again, individual clients—ordinarily not distracted by this abstract issue or made schizoid by its dichotomous quality—do some of each. The appropriateness of blending the two alternatives is grist for the counseling mill, where permutations and combinations of activities in and out of the home can be given deliberate consideration. Clients can thus be assisted substantively with taking those options available to them for use of free time, resultant role adjustments being duly taken into account.

## Working Part-Time for Pay

For some clients, the option of part-time employment may be a transition from full-time employment and its attendant roles. Acting as a decompression chamber, part-time work can help the client avoid the retirement "bends." The retiree's self-concept is preserved, together with the respect of significant others. This work need not be busy-work to kill time: according to Riley and Foner (1968, p. 350), research indicates that older persons "are considerably more likely than younger people to say they *enjoy* their job. . . ." Retired persons can maintain this enjoyment through continued employment.

In choosing this option, the kind of work, and a specific job, client and counselor need to consider the factors mentioned in Chapter 2 as well as any additional ones pertinent to individual planning. Overt and covert motivations for continued employment, the dynamic "fit" of further work into the framework of the family, and the superiority of this option over other options may need consideration. It is equally important to take the physical and other characteristics of the client into account.

The kind of work chosen might build on acquired skills and interests, avocational activities, and physical capabilities. There is also the possibility that psychological needs will be met, such as finally achieving self-actualization or giving service to society. Both these broad needs can be fulfilled at once in suitable work demanding dedication beyond oneself; older persons as well as youthful ones might be assisted in choosing and obtaining part-time work by Vocations for Social Change, Canyon, California 94516.

For other assistance in finding a specific job, the

Employment and Training Administration, U. S. Department of Labor, Washington, D. C. 20210, can be contacted. The Employment and Training Administration has contracted—under its Operation Mainstream—for a number of nationwide projects providing part-time employment for older workers. Forty Plus is a placement service for professionals and executives. Mature Temps is a special placement service for older persons desirous of temporary employment; a succession of temporary jobs might meet particular needs better than steady part-time employment.

Placement difficulties are compounded by the frequent inexperience of older persons in seeking jobs. Their own attitudes toward seeking jobs, as well as employer attitudes and practices, further complicate the situation. "The older worker knows full well the current prejudice against those of his age," point out Lawton and Stewart (1968, p. 10). "He is less aware that he himself shares this prejudice and that he is apt to believe that the employer is right who rejects his application." Counselors help clients deal consciously with such attitudes.

At times employers' attitudes can be eased by counselors who can make job placement a service to them as well as to clients. If they can appreciate being provided with mature, qualified, conscientious workers who fill organizational needs, employers can come to look upon counselors as consultants. To accommodate both client capacities and physical requirements, for example, counselors can suggest simple modifications of job tasks or work flow that may benefit an employer's operations and work force in general (Griew, 1964; Marbach, 1968; U. S. Department of Labor, 1967b).

*Working as a Volunteer*

External forces or internal needs may make paid work less desirable or attainable than volunteer work.

"Technology has served man notice that he must find a home, a new anchorage point for himself, outside the world of work," observed Maddox (1968, p. 360), "certainly by the time of retirement if not before then." As developments in our society restrict opportunities to work for pay for older persons, volunteer opportunities may in some instances be the best prospects.

The need to serve society is often best fulfilled through volunteer work. Pollak (1957, p. 33) underscores "the adjustment of many retired people who find positive experiences in devoting themselves to civic or charitable enterprises.... Concern with others has conquered self-concern." Such a conquest releases psychic and other energies that flow into doubly rewarding work. How unpaid work satisfies client needs is suggested by a study (U. S. Department of Labor, 1969) that found 200 reasons why people volunteered.

Far more numerous than these reasons are opportunities for volunteer work. For facility, these opportunities may be divided into two broad types: (1) Working directly with people being provided some kind of social service and (2) working indirectly through a community agency or national organization providing such service. One or the other of these different outlets for altruism may be more appropriate to a client's capabilities, personality, and related characteristics.

Finding volunteer work is discussed, together with much else about volunteering, in *Retire to Action* (Arthur, 1969). Sources of information and of leads to opportunities include the Administration on Aging, Veterans Administration hospitals and other hospitals, salvage and rehabilitation organizations like Goodwill Industries and the Salvation Army, the American Red Cross, and a host of other agencies. Many communities have not only a United Community Fund or similar organization for collecting and distributing charitable contributions, but also a Volunteer Bureau to serve as a link between opportunities and volunteers.

*Using Free Time Creatively*

While both paid and volunteer work have intrinsic and therapeutic value, work is best viewed for general purposes as a means toward an end rather than an end in itself. It ordinarily provides the wherewithal to do the things one wants to do. One end or outcome of work is therefore the leisure or free time to engage in nonwork activities.

Since the terms work, nonwork, and leisure overlap, free time is the preferable term, relatively free of semantic traps. One trap that many fall into is the notion that anything free is without value. People frequently wait out weekends and vacations for the return to work. Perhaps the most definitive term is just "time," for time is all we have.

These free-wheeling paragraphs on creative use of time may help to stir conceptual cobwebs that often clutter the thinking of clients. Even pertinent poetry would help, one of the most apt being two lines of Rabindranath Tagore:

> God respects me when I work,
> But he loves me when I sing.

Listening to Abe Lincoln might give added perspective: "My father taught me to work, but not to love it. I never did like to work and I don't deny it. I'd rather read, tell stories, crack jokes, talk, laugh—anything but work."

*Avocational* is another term reflecting the primacy of work in the Protestant ethic. It has served well enough in giving some focus to free-time activities, from Donald Super's early study of avocational interest patterns (1940) to the recent work on avocational activities for handicapped persons (Overs, O'Connor, & DeMarco, 1974). Some people associate avocational activities with hobbies, which often have negative implications for older clients. "The word 'hobby' has a distasteful meaning to some people," points out Kathryn Close (1972, p. 18), "They associate it with building ships in bottles, whittling, fancy penmanship, or some other 'idle' pastime."

Once semantic straw men like "idle" and "pastime" have been knocked down, whittling—for example—can be seen as useful in wood carving, whether or not the carvings are sold. Equating productivity with salability is antithetical to pure creativity. Using time creatively can also be either active or passive, regardless of physical participation, as one participates emotionally or intellectually while listening to music or reading books.

There are numerous activities to pursue to make creative use of time. If one loves the outdoors, there are nature walks and bird watching, growing flowers and plants, collecting rocks and shells. To satisfy any artistic sense one can play musical instruments, visit museums and art galleries, go to the theater, crochet and knit, weave rugs. Games such as checkers, chess, and cards can be rewarding. And there is always much to learn simply by writing letters, engaging in conversation, learning a language, attending lectures, and attending to the world around and being attuned to others' feelings and thoughts as well as to one's own.

*Coping with Other Complexities*

This alliterative rubric alludes to nitty-gritty matters like retirement income, housing, health, and legal problems. Counselors must be prepared to assist clients with limited financial resources. "The older population is essentially a low-income group," reports Brotman (1971, p. 8), "even though there are considerable numbers of wealthy among them." The U. S. Department of Labor (1971d, p. 17), suggests one reason for this: "A substantial majority of workers do not obtain any pension coverage, or do not acquire sufficient years of continuous coverage during their entire working life to qualify for a private plan benefit."

Needed financial planning can be facilitated through the use of various printed materials (for example, Arnold, Brock, Ledford, & Richards, 1974; Hunter, 1968; Laas, 1970). These publications and numerous other books, booklets, handbooks, manuals, and guides deal with other complex retirement problems as well. A whole series of retirement guides covering separate topical areas of concern is published by the American Association of Retired Persons, 1909 K Street, N.W., Washington, D. C. 20049.

Such retirement planning materials concentrate a good deal on housing. This troublesome topic raises questions such as whether or not to relocate to a different geographic or climatic area, whether or not to move locally to different living arrangements, whether to rent an apartment or own a home, and many additional dilemmas. A major issue, on which people seem to be about equally divided, is whether to live in a community or setting with others of one's age or to live with people of various chronological ages, thus allowing interaction with younger persons. Since each client must solve these dilemmas individually, the pertinent questions and possible answers in the printed materials can help him or her to weigh the pros and cons.

Questions of health and nutrition are similarly dealt with in various publications, combining science and common sense to yield guidelines to good health habits and eating practices. Beyond sensible behavior to sustain their health, however, clients may need to cope with their attitudes toward health in general and toward their own health. "It is the individual's *own* beliefs about his health (in contrast with medical assessments)," report Riley and Foner (1968, p. 346), "that are most clearly associated with his life satisfaction."

Problems referred to previously in this chapter under "Other Retirement Difficulties"—consumer education, personal safety, and legal affairs—are likewise problems of both client perception and client attitude. Some clients, unconsciously bent on self-destruction, may give little heed to mundane matters of survival. Counselors, dealing differentially as always with individual clients, provide whatever proportions of relevant information and emotional support seem needed.

## SUMMARY

Retirement is a time for which people are reluctant to prepare. Counseling is needed by many people approaching retirement to help them plan for the realities of role adjustments, opportunities for optimal use of time, and decisions regarding housing, health, and other matters of everyday living. Even those who are already retired still cope with similar complexities and can benefit from retirement counseling.

*Chapter 4*

# DYING AND DEATH

Counselors can assist terminally ill persons, suicidal or other self-destructive persons, and the families of such persons. Assistance to families can precede or follow death.

Aging naturally leads to dying, which ends in death. This chronological sequence is the basis for the chapter's title. From a psychological perspective, however, the title could well be reversed, for death conceptually and emotionally precedes dying. Death would be seen as dogging our days and hounding our nights, were we not so fearful of facing it that we keep it out of our minds.

Although death is less taboo a topic than it once was—as is true of venereal disease and other sex-related topics—it is not easily discussed openly. If the unknown generates anxiety and various defenses, death produces the greatest anxieties, since no one alive has ever experienced it. According to Freud, the unconscious cannot tolerate the possibility of one's own death. Such denial is actually a burden, making it difficult for people to deal adequately with death even in the abstract or with other people's deaths.

Scientific inquiry has likewise found it difficult to gain knowledge of death's domain. Medical students start out by cutting up cadavers, but how does a social scientist study the dead? It is not surprising, then, that experts in the field of thanatology find their own limited knowledge deadly. Kastenbaum (1969b, p. 26), laments that "psychological death is a murky, forbidding, and unrewarding area of inquiry. . . ."

Study of dying persons has been somewhat more rewarding, but not entirely successful. The defenses of the dying combined with the defenses of the living confound research findings. "We have not as yet found," LeShan (1969, p. 28) regrets, "a useful way of conceptualizing the life and death forces within the individual."

There are added difficulties for counselors and

other helping professionals who might assist dying persons. In discussing the dying patient, Crane (1970, p. 313) mentions the absence of "norms regarding appropriate behavior toward a person whose death is considered inevitable." In dealing with death from terminal illness, the attendant attitudes of patients/clients and of pertinent others, and the role of counselors, this chapter adopts the positive view of Feder (1965, p. 622): "I don't have any idea how we help a person to die, but I am sure we can do much to help a person to *live* up until the time of death."

Also consistent with that view is the chapter's treatment of suicide, other forms of self-destruction, and the role of counselors. Finally the topic of bereavement is discussed, along with the reactions to death of those who remain, and the role of counselors.

## DYING FROM TERMINAL ILLNESS

Numerous medical conditions could be implicated in patients' particular deaths. The nature and timing of someone's death could also be affected by substantive and symptomatic aspects of specific medical conditions. Counselors need to have some knowledge of the usual course of medical conditions resulting in death.

However, psychological knowledge, understanding individual differences, and sensitivity to interpersonal relations are at the heart of the help counselors can bring to dying patients. As Weisman (1972, p. 123) points out, "given the same disease, patients need not follow the same psychosocial sequences. They do not die in the same way, at the same rate, of the same causes, or within the same context of circumstances." Counselors, knowing that change is a constant in human development, can appreciate and implement Weisman's related comment (1972, p. 123): "People do not necessarily die as they have lived. . . ."

*The Five Stages of Kübler-Ross*

Kübler-Ross (1969), giving less emphasis to the individual variability stressed by Weisman, delineates five stages which dying patients normally experience: denial, anger, bargaining, depression, and acceptance. "Denial, at least partial denial, is used by almost all patients," she states (p. 35), "not only during the first stages of illness or following confrontation, but also later on from time to time." This statement allows for the overlapping of her stages.

"When the first stage of denial cannot be maintained any longer," continues Kübler-Ross (p. 44), "it is replaced by feelings of anger, rage, envy, and resentment." This emotional replacement is accompanied by psychological displacement. Patients cast blame outwardly, becoming angry with anyone and anything— doctors, nurses, other patients, family members, and God.

Kübler-Ross (p. 72), then goes on to her bargaining stage: "If we have been unable to face the sad facts in the first period and have been angry at people and God in the second phase, maybe we can succeed in entering into some sort of an agreement which may postpone the inevitable happening. . . ." Patients may bargain with God for a little more time by promising some kind of good behavior, in the manner of children who wish to stay up later. They beseech physicians, not unlike gods to patients, to postpone death in exchange, for example, for bequests of parts of the body to science.

In the fourth stage Kübler-Ross distinguishes two types of depression: a reactive depression resulting from a sense of past loss and a preparatory depression anticipating impending loss. Past loss may include physical health, parts of the body, employment, finances, role within the family, and other personally perceived deprivations. Impending loss of everything and especially of people causes a preparatory depression that confronts an ephemeral future. However, this anticipatory stage may more readily lead to the final stage of acceptance.

"Acceptance should not be mistaken for a happy stage," cautions Kübler-Ross (p. 100), "It is almost void of feelings." Nor is it (p. 99), "a resigned and hopeless 'giving up,' a sense of 'what's the use' or 'I just cannot fight it any longer'. . . ." With the preceding stages out of their system, as it were, patients are realistically prepared for what is to come. Kübler-Ross makes the point, however, that some patients reach this stage prematurely. They already accept what might be prevented or postponed had they a less yielding attitude.

*Attitudinal Variations on a Theme*

The Kübler-Ross paradigm is a useful model for understanding the attitudes of dying persons, just as life stages or psychosocial phases help to understand persons presumably not so close to death. Erikson's eight ages (1963) similarly culminate in ego integrity that dissipates potential despair in the face of death. Fear of death gives way to acceptance and "death loses its sting" (p. 268).

The Kübler-Ross stages do not meet with the complete acceptance, however, of all other thanatological experts. "One does not find a unidirectional movement through progressive stages," suggests Shneidman (1973, p. 7), "so much as an alternation between acceptance and denial." Feifel (1973) reports finding in many dying persons simultaneous acceptance and rejection of death.

Such simultaneity resembles the psychophysical phenomenon wherein two presented odors are perceived at the same time. The same presentation may result in perceiving first one odor and then the other. This is comparable to the theory of alternating perception expressed by Shneidman (1973). Just as one odor may also mask the other, acceptance of death may be a cover-up for what is regarded as socially unacceptable denial. Another possibility applicable to odors—blending the two into something totally different—may apply to positive and negative attitudes toward death. The integration of these attitudes perhaps parallels Erikson's ego integrity.

Denial is undoubtedly the most pervasive and persistent of responses to dying. Whether death-denying is also death-defying, denial expresses itself in different ways. These range from the verbal and highly explicit to the verbal and evasive to the nonverbal but visually or aurally almost explicit. An example of the verbal-evasive is speaking of one's dying as though it is happening to someone else, a survival strategy made familiar by Frankl (1963).

Numerous dynamics underlie patients' attitudes toward dying. Whether patients lean toward denial or acceptance, and the extent to which they exemplify anger, bargaining, and depression, might depend on whether their locus of control is external or internal. Do they attribute control over their lives to God and others or to themselves?

State anxiety versus trait anxiety might similarly affect the different ways in which patients cope with dying. Succumbing, incidentally, is properly regarded as a form of coping, given credence by the acceptability of acceptance. Without invoking Freud's concept of castration anxiety or simply of separation anxiety, discomfort over impending death could, with some patients, be an extension *in extremis* of their characteristic anxiety. Yet patients in whom situations induce anxiety may be demonstrating not so much anxiety as realistic fear of death.

## Medical and Familial Dilemmas

One dilemma confronting families is *where* will the dying patient die. As Feifel (1973) points out most patients in our society do leave their homes for hospitals, convalescent homes, and nursing homes. The veritable disintegration of the extended family pushes dying people out of the homes in which most would prefer to stay. The decision the family makes concerning where the dying patient will go hinges on the cost of terminal illness, the care required, and mixed emotions of resentment and guilt. These factors also affect the focus and flavor of further interactions of the family with the patient.

Families and physicians share a dilemma regarding the possible prolongation of life and the purposeful cessation of life. Ethical questions abound in this area. Who knows when someone who is "alive" is no longer *living*? When do the patient's "right to die" (Group for the Advancement of Psychiatry, 1974) and the principle of euthanasia properly predominate over the principle of "live and let live"? Saunders (1969, p. 52) makes a distinction between "prolonging living" and "prolonging dying," but who can determine that fine demarcation on the continuum of life from the beginning till its end?

A major dilemma with particular implications for counselors has to do with telling patients and families about terminal illness. There is the basic question of "To tell or not to tell?" According to Feifel (1965, p. 635), most terminal patients want to be told, whereas most physicians prefer not to tell. Whether because of time constraints or their own death anxieties, physicians tend to relegate this responsibility to nurses or families. However, others may not pick up the ball, if only that telling goes counter to their own inner inclinations.

Not that all patients should be told. Wahl (1973), after presenting pros and cons of telling patients, concludes (p. 19) that "if you try to reduce so important a matter in patient care to an invariable maxim, you can do an incredible amount of harm." In another consideration of individual differences, a physician's suggestion is reported (Bowers, Jackson, Knight, & LeShan, 1964, p. 103) that "when the question, 'Should the patient be told the truth?' is raised, we ask, 'Pray, which patient and what truth?'"

Shneidman (1973) further refines the questions and also reflects the perplexities in trying to answer them: "The professional literature dealing with the dying— what to tell, how much to tell, how to tell, when to tell, whom to tell—is somewhat confusing if not contradictory . . ." (p. 30). There is confusion as to whether or to reveal diagnoses or prognoses. Most writers seem to agree that whatever is told should be told in relation to a patient's capacity to absorb the information and at a rate appropriate to the individual.

*Counselors Deal with Dying*

In view of the various attitudes toward dying and the difficult dilemmas confronting families and professionals, counselors face a special challenge in assisting dying persons. The challenge can be surmounted, however, if counselors have some understanding of pertinent principles and dynamics, self-understanding with respect to dying and death, and sensitivity to interactions with dying persons and significant others. Since sensitive counselors base most of their understanding upon vicarious learning, one need not be literally dying oneself to be an effective counselor.

As Saunders emphasizes (1969, p. 78), *"you learn the care of the dying from the dying themselves."*

Falsely dichotomizing patients and counselors, who

are simply at different points on a continuum, gives rise to misconceptions regarding communication. "The dying and the living do not speak the same language," platitudinizes the playwright Schnitzler, "and there is little they can communicate to each other." With empathy made accurate by knowing the attitude of a patient, a counselor who listens and observes learns what the patient is saying verbally and nonverbally, and can respond in kind. Nonverbal responses to dying persons may include tactual ones such as holding the person's hand to touch his or her feelings and show that someone cares.

Mundane matters must often be dealt with, as patients want to leave things in order for their families. They may require assistance regarding financial arrangements, burial or cremation, bequests of body or specific organs, and distribution prior to death of particular possessions with monetary or sentimental value. Part of the challenge to counselors is to be not only sensitive but also sensible.

As they prepare to depart this world, many patients are concerned about dying without psychological closure. Not all believe, with St. Francis of Assisi, that "it is in dying that we are born to eternal life." Carey (1974) found little relationship between the emotional adjustment of terminal patients and their religious orientation. The apparent attrition of traditional religion, the diminishing acceptance of an afterlife, and indeed the belief that "God is dead" have weakened some earlier sources of solace for the dying.

Yet a variety of Wordsworth's "intimations of immortality" may be introduced, by patient or counselor, into the search for serenity. The poet Horace's "Not all of me will die" can be realized not only by the material things one leaves or bequeathes (money, property, heirlooms, creative works, letters, photographs, recordings, transplants) but also by numerous intangibles. One lives on in the lives of others through one's descendants, genetically as well as in their memories. One goes on living in the hearts of friends and acquaintances. And one's influence is still alive in other persons whose lives one has touched such as co-workers, customers, students, patients, spectators, co-members of organizations. One may say, with Tennyson's Ulysses, "I am a part of all that I have met." One's body remains a part of the universe, as matter is never lost.

In all serious discussions, as in this presentation, there is always room for humor. Humor and laughter provide a natural release of anxiety. Perhaps that result justifies certain responses sometimes made to patients' perpetual question, "Will I die?" At least one physician is supposed to have responded, "Die! That's the last thing in the world you'll do." A gentler gibe has been: "Yes, of course, and so will I." This twist on Browning's optimism in "Rabbi Ben Ezra" ("The best is yet to be. . . .") may undercut some patients' complaints: "Cheer up! The worst is yet to come."

Whether or not humor is appropriate with the families of dying patients, counselors need to work with families in serving dying clients. In addition to physical death and psychological death, there is social death, which seems related to removal from the home and loss of close contact with family members and friends. The counselor can act as a liaison to facilitate the maintenance of contact, as well as the efficient ordering of final family matters. Family counseling can also alleviate anticipatory grief (Doyle, 1972) and lighten the later burden of bereavement.

## TAKING ONE'S OWN LIFE

Self-destruction is a form of death so pervasive that most counselors at some time or other deal with persons who are in the process of taking their own lives. The process may be acute and accomplished quickly or it may be chronic and long drawn out. Suicide occurs in so many guises that all its occurrences are not reported. Thus, statistics understate the incidence and prevalence of suicide in our society.

Society's generally negative view of suicide as reflected by the false reports of families, police, and others helps to keep the statistics down. "This way," admitted one police chief (Grollman, 1971, p. 8), "we spare the family the terrible disgrace." The shame which stigmatizes suicide as a dishonorable discharge from life may also serve as a deterrent. However, in other parts of the world hara-kiri and other methods of self-destruction have a more honorable social status. This suggests that suicide is perhaps not inherently evil but subject to social evaluation.

In the growing literature on suicide there is much evidence of social evaluation together with personal biases of particular writers. There is the notion of suicide as a crime against the State, expressed at least since Aristotle and widely implemented through legislation. This concept is sometimes displaced into diagnostic terms that seem to conclude, "To commit suicide, one has to be crazy." One, maybe, but not all. Consider the high incidence of suicides at most age levels, particularly among aging persons (Batchelor, 1957), who do not necessarily lose their mental or emotional marbles.

It is easy for authors to lose their professional perspective, for suicide touches everyone to the quick. The same unconscious motivations that lead to some suicides may be operating in some authors, causing either compassion and absolution or reaction formation and condemnation. Societal and personal prejudices hamper the search for understanding of suicidal behavior and can keep suicidology from becoming a science.

*What Makes Suicides Run?*

In a too narrow "search for the suicidal personality," Cantor (1970) found "a remarkably complex picture of possible causal factors" (p. 64). Compared to unidimensional explanations, multicausality emerges from the literature and from experience as a more parsimonious approach to the many syndromes of suicide. A suicidal personality is no more likely than an alcoholic personality or an epileptic personality. Grinker (1967) seems closer to the mark in concluding that there is "a variety of clinical entities, of situations, and/or personality characteristics associated with suicide" (p. 62).

Adopting a broad approach to suicide within "the psychology of death," Kastenbaum and Aisenberg (1972) first posited certain "reasons" that people commit suicide (p. 251):

1. being psychotic and not knowing what they are doing
2. acting on impulse and not thinking about the future
3. feeling discomfort so acute that they care about nothing but escape
4. believing they are already dying and have no earthly future
5. believing that the future will be no better or even worse
6. feeling that what they can gain symbolically through death is more important than anything continued life can offer
7. generally feeling that life has no meaning.

Seeking causes underlying such reasons, Kastenbaum and Aisenberg then reviewed (pp. 252–276) the relationships between suicide and the following variables: age, sex, race, subcultural group membership, marital status, socioeconomic level, mental illness, and suicide preventatives (objects, situations, or events that interfere with the initiation or completion of suicidal acts). The authors (p. 252) warn that whoever expects the relationships of "at least some of the variables to be simple, direct, and easily understood is doomed to disappointment."

The identification of both dependence and independence as needs that drive people to suicide illustrates the complexity of possible causes. Just as the same need operates differently in different people, divergent needs may converge in the same outcome. Dependence is readily apparent in suicide following the death of one upon whom the suicide was dependent. Independence appears related to the finding (Crane, p. 311) "that people would prefer to control their mode of dying, . . . that they would like to be able to maintain as much control as possible over their deaths." The struggle of many individuals for independence from society and their parents may symbolize a central concern for control over their own lives, including their own deaths. Close to this concept is Feifel's perception (1957, p. 56): "Birth is an uncontrolled event but the manner of one's departure from life may bear a definite relation to one's philosophy of life and death."

### Self-Destructive Behavior

For counselors, theoretical conceptualizations regarding self-destruction can be a basis for understanding and helping suicidal clients. Counselors also need more pragmatic approaches to recognize suicidal bents through self-destructive behavior. If causes are to be eliminated or alleviated, behavioral symptoms, signs, and signals must become familiar as indices of underlying psychodynamics. Such dynamics may be both intrapsychic and interpersonal (Sullivan, 1953).

Indices to be observed can be placed in two rather rough categories. The first category includes *conscious, intentional* behavior geared toward *direct* suicide and *instant* death. In the other category, behavior is basically *unconscious, subintentional,* and leading to *indirect* suicide over a *prolonged* period. These differential behaviors representing different client dynamics may suggest differential counseling strategies to avert death.

Actual attempts to commit suicide are obvious indices in the first category of conscious, intentional behavior. They are nevertheless disregarded by some counselors and other professionals who overlook the obvious to probe deeply into the client's unconscious. It is wiser and safer practice to give heed to such common conscious behavior as suicide attempts and verbal threats.

Nonverbal signs and emotional symptoms may overlap the two categories, depending in part upon the intent and awareness of a particular client. Such behavior as giving away prized possessions may speak loudly of potential suicide. Other signals are depression and related emotions, accompanied by behavior at reduced or heightened energy levels.

Attempts, threats, aberrant behavior, and emotion/energy swings may separately or totally make up an intentional or subintentional "cry for help" (Farberow and Shneidman, 1961). An "unsuccessful" attempt at suicide frequently succeeds in getting others to hear the muffled cry. Counselors with sensitized antennae, including "the third ear" (Reik, 1949), can pick up communications crucial in identifying suicidal individuals.

Equally important to counselors are indices for indirect suicide of extended duration—"slow suicide," in popular parlance. Rome (1970, p. 48) mentions "cryptosuicides: those persons whose self-destructive behavior is partly masked by taking place over a prolonged period." Such persons engage in a wide (and wild) range of unconscious, subintentional suicidal behavior. They may drive "like crazy," are more than "accident-prone," repeatedly risk their lives, abuse alcohol and other drugs, and even provoke others to kill them.

Grollman (1971), in a rare gem of printing expertise as well as prime scholarship, sums up "clues to people with the greatest suicide predisposition" (p. 83): previous suicide attempt, direct or disguised threat, chronic illness or isolation, bereavement, financial stress, domestic difficulties, severe depression, psychosis, alcoholism, abuse of drugs, family history of suicide. He also emphasizes the current role of the (sometimes suicidogenic) family.

*Counselors Confront Suicide*

The role counselors play with respect to suicide critically illustrates issues that pertain to counseling in general. Persons identified as suicidal are indeed to be treated "with respect," regardless of the social and personal biases encountered in the professional literature on suicide. Counselors need not have attempted suicide themselves to understand, both cognitively and affectively, client "reasons," underlying motivations, and shifting moods.

"Confront" in the above heading does not mean the use of confrontation solely to have clients face up to their inadequacies. Suicidal clients who are easily put down and put upon by "helping" professionals, need such "treatment" even less than most other clients. Clients bent on suicide can profit from confrontation with their strong points, with positive interpersonal patterns, and with reasons for living based on their own needs and the needs of others.

The emphasis on family counseling in the section on dealing with dying persons also applies to suicidal persons. "The needs, goals, and strivings of the significant others must be taken into account," stresses Grollman. "One must understand the emotional climate of the family before he can understand the individual member" (1971, pp. 78–79). Indeed, the family rather than the individual may be the stimulus to self-destruction. The suicidal response, on the other hand, often stems from misperceived emotions or misinterpreted attitudes that clear up in the course of family counseling. Should suicide nevertheless occur, the family is better prepared for that event and its consequences.

The external stimulus to self-destruction may be outside the family proper. Wherever it is or whoever it is, Jourard maintains (1972, p. 49) that "a person destroys himself in response to an invitation originating from others that he stop living." Jourard sees society as inviting people to do away with themselves by maintaining false values that sick or aging persons find hard to live up to. Other individuals, too, subtly or openly invite people to "drop dead." Counselors should heed Jourard's insistence (p. 49) that "a person *lives* in response to the experience of repeated invitations to continue living."

A final reminder worth repeating is that counselors must attempt to keep their own values (never false to them) out of true counseling of clients, so that the process is not one of dogmatic indoctrination. Although Grollman (1971) is a rabbi, he warns against moralizing (p. 87) or being angry (p. 89) with suicidal clients. Counselors might profit from the highly pertinent philosophy succinctly expressed by Neale (1973, p. 67): "Suicide can be prevented only by permitting it."

## BEREAVEMENT

Those who are left when people die generally feel a sense of loss. Even impersonal scanning of the obituary column induces a bereft feeling, albeit commonly mixed with a subliminal savor of survival. Even the most secure of survivors recognize that the bell tolls for them, too. It is not surprising, then, that bereavement for most is a time of bitterness, though for some it may be bittersweet.

Reactions to death, while they may follow a general pattern, can also be widely diverse in their nature, sequence, depth, and visibility. This section discusses typical and perhaps some atypical reactions to death, the variables involved, and the role of counselors in dealing with persons bereaved or presumably bereaved. If the words "presumably" and "bittersweet" appear ambiguous, they will become clarified as dynamic variables are discussed.

### Variables Affecting Reactions to Death

It is usually presumed that a person left behind by someone's death is "bereaved," that is, deprived of something valuable. The first variable, however, in the list presented by Hickey and Szabo (1973, p. 6) is "the degree of importance the deceased had in the life of the survivor. . . ." The "loss of a loved one" is not always suffered by those left behind. Custom and socially acceptable behavior, indeed, seem to underlie the prescribed presumption and conforming reactions. Sudnow (1967, p. 142) makes a similar point: "Bereaved persons must be cognizant of the fact that for others their bereavement may be more relevant than it is for themselves."

The Hickey-Szabo list continues with these variables:

1. how others react to the death
2. the ages of the deceased and the bereaved

3.  the physical and emotional state of the bereaved
4.  reactions to prior death experiences
5.  the value structure of the family
6.  the number of dominant friendships experienced
7.  the security and stability of early relationships in the home setting
8.  the particular timing of the death and related circumstances
9.  changes in lifestyle and role necessitated by the death
10. the degree of resulting dependency.

Particular combinations and permutations of variables give idiosyncratic identity to the individual survivor's reactions, within the normative limits of social constraints. Formal norms such as funerals, wakes, the wearing of black, and other familiar rituals have given way to less formal and more ambiguous ground rules, more open to individual interpretation. To some extent, as Krupp and Kligfeld point out (1973, p. 144), "the deritualization of American culture tends to throw the mourner upon his own resources. . . ."

*How Survivors React to Death*

Emotional as well as physical shock is a common initial reaction. A numbness sometimes sets in that also impairs the intellectual processes. Mainly emotional, however, the reactions run the gamut from guilt to resentment. Mixed emotions or confused feelings frequently characterize reactions to death.

There may be guilt feelings rather than guilt, which implies actual culpability of some kind in the surviving person. Guilt might apply to a survivor whose faulty driving, for example, caused the accidental death of the deceased. Survivors may have guilt feelings, on the other hand, about any number of perceived errors of commission or omission during the life of the deceased, especially toward the end. These feelings are particularly likely if the deceased is a suicide. Feeling guilty about the death itself can be one of the most shattering reactions.

Resentment, anger, and even envy often ensue as reactions to death. Blame may be cast upon the deceased for dying, as though it were some spiteful stratagem. Survivors who had expected to die first may feel cheated. A sense of envy sometimes arises because the other died instead of oneself, sometimes because the deceased is overidealized through eulogies and the doctrine of saying "nothing but good about the dead."

Some emotional reactions are muted by social constraints. People tend to be careful of expressing any sense of relief they may feel, be it because the prolonged suffering of a deceased person is over or personal and financial strain is gone. Even less to be revealed is glee that a no-good is gone. Composure is safer, being a reaction more compatible with cultural norms. Subcultural norms, incidentally, differ from group to group and need to be taken into account by counselors.

Grief and mourning are regarded not only as reactions to death but as an essential phase of the process of recovery. While composure is countenanced culturally, professionals in the field generally emphasize the therapeutic benefits of cathartic venting of emotions. Survivors are to do their "grief work" and complete "the work of mourning" if they are to snap back to their former selves.

Although many survivors are better off not bottling up their emotions, to overgeneralize the necessity for grief and mourning may be to oversimplify the situation for others. The very terminology, stressing "work" and "working through," suggests a parallel to the work ethic and its well-known expectations and implications. Some survivors take the "job" so seriously that they display feigned grief. For some survivors catharsis of grief occurred during the deceased's course of dying. Working to express emotions may be more natural, on the other hand, for those who have repressed their feelings to simulate composure.

Ambiguities in the interpretation of sociocultural norms, ambivalence of emotions, strength of emotions and of control over them, and repeated bereavements may create almost unbearable emotional burdens. Kastenbaum's concept of a "bereavement overload" (1969a, p. 51) with aging persons experiencing a succession of losses appears applicable to other persons made vulnerable by death and its aftermath. Not uncommon is early death of survivors, sometimes by suicide. Lasagna (1970, p. 80) mentions the elevated mortality of bereaved persons within 1 year of bereavement.

*Counselors and Bereavement*

The complexities underlying and pervading reactions to death suggest that counselors avoid simplistic interpretation of reactions and superficial treatment of clients. Counselors need to be sophisticated at least beyond pigeon-holing all survivors as sorely bereaved and administering sympathy and optimism as adequate restoratives.

As Paul points out (1969), survivors receive an abundance of sympathy from relatives and friends. What helping professionals can provide is empathy. Counselors are enabled to empathize with survivors not only on the basis of personal experiences with death, but also on the basis of vicarious learnings from professional experiences. These experiences include a study of human behavior within social contexts and work with a variety of clients at different age levels.

As in other areas of counseling, some people concerned give great weight to the counselor's having undergone the same experience as the client. The perceived correlation between a common experience and counseling expertise is the basis for widow-to-widow programs. While widows and widowers can no doubt be effective in helping those recently widowed, the shared experience does not assure success.

Emphasis must be placed on the value of counseling the prospective survivors prior to the impending death. Alleviation of anticipatory or premortem grief may leave little "working through" of postmortem grief to be accomplished. Although this approach is not applicable to most instances of sudden death, it can often be applied to situations where suicide is the outcome. The warning signals that frequently precede suicide give families and counselors an opportunity to forestall the unhappy ending or, when prevention and intervention fail, to accomplish some of the grief work required during what is called postvention (Grollman, 1971).

Counseling with survivors also parallels and profits from prior counseling they received with the dying person. The "meaning" of the death or of death in general, for example, is a matter of concern during the period the person is dying and continues to be so after the person has died. Again, counseling might deal in part with such "intimations of immortality" as seem to make sense with particular clients.

Much of post-death counseling deals, however, with more mundane matters, some of them similar to those that entered into pre-death counseling. To assist counselors and survivors in coping with the numerous details related to death, free material is provided by some funeral parlors, banks, insurance companies, and other sources of practical information. Books edited by Grollman (1974) and Kutscher (1969) contain chapters on such down-to-earth matters as burial versus cremation, organ donation and transplantation, funerals, choosing cemeteries and memorials, mourning rituals, condolence calls and sympathy letters, insurance and legal affairs, family financial management, and even handling of pets.

## SUMMARY

Dying arouses a wide range of reactions in those dying, in members of the family, and in helping personnel. Counselors can assist dying persons and their families—the latter before and after death—with regard to attitudinal and other adjustments. Suicidal behavior, whether intentional or indirect, can be dealt with by counselors sensitive to the dynamics of self-destruction.

*Chapter 5*

# TRENDS, ISSUES, AND RECOMMENDATIONS

Counseling older persons is most effectively offered by personnel knowledgeable about social contexts, legislative directions, and needed developments.

Counseling older persons in regard to careers, retirement, dying, or death can profit from perspective as well as expertise, just as a ground sets off a figure. Recent trends and contemporary developments, together with persisting issues and suggested directions, may give depth as well as breadth to the substantive services offered older clients.

Effective counseling can scarcely occur in a vacuum, which is naturally abhorred by counselors who appreciate clients' constant interaction with external realities. Toward maximization of their services, counselors not only work knowledgeably within existing environmental realities, but also strive for needed environmental modifications. Counselors can bring about social changes of ultimate benefit to clients when they act as advocates in the professional role and as activists in their role of citizens.

This final chapter presents some of the kinds of information counselors need to enhance their awareness of trends and issues and perhaps to raise their social consciousness regarding the problems of older persons. Three appendixes add supplementary information: these are selective lists of (1) readings related to older women, (2) periodicals pertinent to older persons, and (3) organizations concerned with older persons.

## TRENDS

Progress has been made in recent years with respect to both the problems and the potentials of older persons. Society has recognized its elder citizens through relevant

conferences and through responsive legislative enactments to establish or support agencies and programs
geared to provide needed services. A brief review follows
of some of the significant conferences, legislative acts,
and agencies and programs.

*Older Persons Acknowledged*

It is significant, first of all, that acknowledgment or recognition of the substantial segment of older persons in
the population, which has emerged only since 1961,
must be recorded as a mark of progress.

In 1961 the first White House Conference on Aging
was held, a high-water mark in the tidal surge arising
after years of stagnation. Adopted at the 1961 White
House Conference on Aging was the following Senior
Citizen's Charter:

*Rights of Senior Citizens*

Each senior citizen, regardless of race, color, or creed, is
entitled to the RIGHT to:
1.  Be useful.
2.  Obtain employment based on merit.
3.  Freedom from want in old age.
4.  A fair share of the community's recreational,
    educational, and medical resources.
5.  Obtain decent housing suited to the needs of
    later years.
6.  The moral and financial support of one's family
    so far as is consistent with the best interest of
    the family.
7.  Live independently as one chooses.
8.  Live and die with dignity.
9.  Access to all available knowledge on how to
    improve the later years of life.

Although these rights are far from having been achieved, they were not specifically reaffirmed or expanded in any similar Bill of Rights resulting from the 1971 White House Conference on Aging. Since each of these two high-water marks, however, sufficient ferment has arisen to activate legislation for the rights of senior citizens. The 1971 conference itself produced numerous recommendations, some already implemented.

Among the most significant legislative enactments have been the Older Americans Act, the Age Discrimination in Employment Act, the Employee Retirement Income Security Act, the Housing and Community Development Act, and an act to provide community service employment for older workers. Medicare and Medicaid were created to furnish health services to older persons. A National Institute on Aging was established within the National Institutes of Health to foster research on aging. The Department of Health, Education, and Welfare now includes an Administration on Aging with an Area-Agency-on-Aging network for national planning and coordination of pertinent programs.

The legislative and executive branches of the federal government have demonstrated recognition of the older population. The Senate has a Special Committee on Aging, with subcommittees on housing for the elderly, employment and retirement incomes, federal/state/community services, consumer interests of the elderly, health of the elderly, retirement and the individual, and long-term care. More recently established in the House of Representatives is a Select Committee on Aging. By proclamation of the President, May has been designated Older Americans Month.

In a booklet on supplemental income, The Social Security Administration (1973) recognizes the continuing needs of older persons by making these points: in 1900 one in 25 was over 65 years of age, and the life expectancy was 45 years, whereas in 1972 one in ten was over 65, with life expectancy at 72 years; a longer life uses up reserves as inflation affects fixed incomes and medical costs rise with the increase of health problems; and changing social attitudes force retirement at earlier ages, disrupt patterns of living, and loosen family ties. Just as supplemental income cannot deter all these trends, one month to honor older Americans cannot compensate for eleven months of dishonor.

## Agencies and Programs

Despite incomplete recognition of older Americans manifested in equally fragmented programs, there has been progress. The evidence is in the increased quantity and quality of services available such as the thousands of multipurpose senior centers in operation across the country. Retirement preparation programs have multiplied in both public and private employment. Suicide prevention centers, widow-to-widow programs, and multidisciplinary gerontology centers have grown. The number and variety of continuing education opportunities for older persons have also increased. Even a National Senior Citizens Law Center has been established, to deal with the legal problems of the elderly poor.

Since a large proportion of the older population seeks employment, either for added income or for added edification, programs of various kinds have developed to meet these aims. Employment for pay is the purpose of such programs as those conducted, as part of Operation Mainstream, under contract with the Employment and Training Administration of the U. S. Department of Labor. Pay is involved in some of the programs conducted directly by the federal agency called ACTION. Unfortunately, because this agency has been used as a political football, it and its programs may not be functioning at the time this material is being read. Its programs have included the Foster Grandparent Program, the Senior Companion Program, the Retired Senior Volunteer Program (RSVP), the Service Corps of Retired Executives (SCORE), Volunteers in Service to America (VISTA), the Peace Corps, and ACTION Cooperative Volunteers.

Unpaid volunteer work for older persons is available through numerous programs, agencies, and other settings. Programs that serve older persons, such as senior citizen centers, also offer opportunities for volunteer service. Volunteers constitute the backbone of many community agencies referred to as voluntary agencies. Y's and health associations and minority organizations are among the settings open to volunteer workers. A multiminority organization with opportunities for volunteers is Women in Community Service (WICS), 1730 Rhode Island Avenue, N.W., Washington, D. C. 20036. Appendix 3 lists organizations concerned with older persons that may directly or indirectly provide opportunities for volunteer work.

## ISSUES

The favorable trends manifested by the recognition accorded older persons and the progress evident in available programs are still far outnumbered by unresolved critical issues. Underlying the specific issues to be mentioned are society's general attitudes toward aging and toward death. These natural stages of life arouse vague apprehension and anxiety which are displaced upon innocent individuals who happen to be aging and dying. With suicide already labeled a crime, perhaps society would some day label aging and dying as crimes.

Societal attitudes are also revealed, somewhat paradoxically, in terms like "senior citizen" and "golden years." Many older persons and gerontologists regard these terms as euphemisms thinly gilding gray realities with a spurious optimism. "Senior citizen" can be doubly faulted: besides the sugarcoating "senior" the other exclusionary word seems to eliminate noncitizens from society's proper concern for all human beings.

## Employment and Retirement

The legislation enacted in recent years did not include a bill that would have established midcareer development services for middle-aged and older workers. Under such a bill, unemployed and underemployed persons 45 and older would have been provided training, counseling, and other supportive services by the U. S. Department of Labor. The current Comprehensive Employment and Training Act (CETA) carries no mandate for services to older workers. Second career planning and implementation require legislative and programmatic backing to convert a more or less haphazard trend into a significant societal advance.

The legislation to put an end to age discrimination in employment needs to be strictly enforced. The act itself is inadequate in citing 65 as the last age protected from discrimination. Employers stop capable workers below that age from gaining employment through devious pretexts for rejection. Any age is an inappropriate criterion on which to base eligibility for employment, insurance, credit, or other benefits.

Similarly, age ought not to be an inflexible basis for mandatory retirement. Rather than force retirement upon older workers, employers could offer various forms of flexible, gradual, or trial retirement. Employers could also offer incentives for late retirement as opposed to early retirement, since many employees continue to be competent in their work long after the usual retirement ages.

Retirement preparation needs to include more counseling, with individuals and groups, as a supplement to the "education" approach conducted in a classroom atmosphere. The concept of continuing education also needs to be broadened beyond academic courses to all kinds of training and retraining that will fill gaps in skills and knowledge as well as strengthen prior competencies. Manual skills, too often treated as second-class abilities, offer the possibility of prolonged life, for Gallup (1974, pp. 109–110) reports a relationship between continuing to work with one's hands and longevity.

*Where and How People Live*

A major issue concerns the merits of retirement communities versus housing that integrates older and younger persons. Some retired persons prefer to spend their time with other older persons, feeling comfortable in conversations or activities that reflect broadly shared experiences. The "birds of a feather" concept ruffles the feathers of other retired persons, who find talk and games with chronological peers stultifying and contacts with young persons stimulating. Legislation and funding can resolve this dilemma by providing housing to accommodate both alternatives.

Also to be considered in the design and provision of housing for older persons are alternative living arrangements in relation to families. Again, some retired persons prefer to remain with their families in whatever kinds of dwellings can physically accommodate such extended families. Other retired persons recognize that psychological accommodations or adjustments often are not compatible with extended family living arrangements. They accept the newer nuclear family concept and opt for settling nearby.

Nearby facilities of many types can afford older persons the convenience of needed social, recreational, educational, and other activities. Multipurpose senior centers located in urban, suburban, small town, and rural areas can meet these needs, if adequate funding is legislatively appropriated and otherwise supplemented. Senior centers could extend their services by reaching out to lower socioeconomic segments of the population. They could expand their services by imaginatively developing activities for creative use of time.

## Where and How People Die

Some of the same variables which affect where older persons live also affect where they die. And where they die affects how they die. It may make a difference to them whether they die among family members, old friends, young friends, or strangers. The best way the living can try to understand the dying is by thinking of "them" as "us."

Geographic mobility and social mobility, as well as the breakdown of the extended family, have separated a large proportion of older persons from those who are dear to them. The consequent aloneness and feeling of loneliness while living are perhaps only exceeded by the aloneness and loneliness of dying. What might otherwise sound commonplace and even corny, therefore, carries human poignancy and social sense: "The family that lives together dies together."

Pertinent issues are raised by Kastenbaum and Aisenberg (1972, pp. 479–481) in a series of sensitive questions regarding the increased prevalence of dying in hospitals:

Is the dying process important enough to us to stimulate the development of more adequate and humanistic care? ... Is it best to reintegrate dying with the larger community? ... How feasible is it to develop mobile and flexible systems to support dying at home? ... Should not the dying person be some place where he is wanted and valued?

## RECOMMENDATIONS

Since the trends and issues have not been discussed with complete dispassion, compassion being essential to concern over critical junctures in life, some recommendations have been at least implicit in the presentation. Explicit recommendations regarding matters of concern in this monograph have been developed in recent years in relation to the 1971 White House Conference on Aging. This concluding section presents three major sources of recommendations proposed subsequent to the conference, several recommendations prepared prior to the conference, and selected recommendations resulting from the conference itself.

Among the major sources of current recommendations is the Special Committee on Aging of the United States Senate. The Committee issues updated reports on developments regarding aging (for example, 1974), together with recommendations and minority views. Also, the American Association of Retired Persons/ National Retired Teachers Association prepares detailed recommendations for implementation at both national and state levels (for example, 1974). And The National Council on the Aging summarizes relevant social developments and suggests responsive policies and practices (for example, Quirk, 1974).

As part of a position paper for the 1971 White

House Conference on the Aging, the National Council on the Aging prepared several recommendations pertaining to employment. Apparently these recommendations, which aimed for a national policy to assure middle-aged and older workers opportunities for continued employment, were not adopted by the conference. It was proposed (pp. 8–9) that techniques for relating the functional abilities of workers to the functional requirements of jobs be used as an alternative to judging ability to perform specific work tasks by chronological age; retraining programs be expanded to update obsolete skills; training programs for employers be instituted on how to recognize, value, and utilize the skills and potential skills of middle-aged and older workers; second career approaches be expanded, particularly in the human services; and work and jobs be designed around people to achieve the flexibility required to accommodate workers of different ages, skills, and capability levels.

Recommendations pertinent to employment that were adopted by the 1971 White House Conference on Aging (Subcommittee on Aging of the Committee on Labor and Public Welfare and Special Committee on Aging, United States Senate, 1973) include the following, among many others:

> Federal, State, and local governments should strictly enforce protective and anti-discriminatory laws and policies regarding employment opportunities, with the elimination of the age limit of 65 in age discrimination legislation. The age discrimination act of 1967 should be expanded to cover all employees in both private and public sectors. (p. 255)

All the remaining recommendations come from the same source. Selected recommendations that pertain to retirement follow:

Society should adopt a policy of preparation for retirement, leisure, and education for life off the job.... Retirement and leisure time planning begins with the early years and continues through life.... While retirement preparation is both an individual and total community responsibility, every employer has a major responsibility for providing preparation-for-retirement programs during the working hours. (p. 536)

A flexible (retirement) policy should be adopted based upon the worker's desires and needs and upon his physical and mental capacity. (p. 259)

Education, in both broad and narrow senses, is emphasized in a number of recommendations, such as the following:

Emphasis should be placed on including curricula or course contents on physical, mental, and social aspects of aging in secondary schools, undergraduate professional education, and in inservice training and continuing education of health personnel. The development of specialists in the care of the elderly should also receive emphasis, especially with the view of developing professional, allied health professional, and other health personnel selected and trained to give compassionate and expert care to the aged. (p. 429)

In addition, emphasis should be placed on the development of community college level certificate and degree programs and programs in vocational and technical institutes as well as other local programs for personnel who deliver services to the older population. Teacher training programs should include positive concepts regarding the aging process and the older person for incorporation into elementary and secondary school curricula. (p. 518)

Appropriate materials and methods about all aspects of aging must be developed and introduced in the curricula at all levels of education from preschool through higher education. (p. 240)

A continuing national program for education of all

persons should be provided about the specific physical, mental, and social aspects of aging. Educational programs should be addressed to all ages and should include all stages of development so that the different age groups will better understand each other. . . . The aged themselves should be among those recruited, trained, and utilized in carrying out these programs. (p. 427)

Involvement between young people and older people should be encouraged at all levels of community life. Young people can gain knowledge of the process of aging and become involved with elderly people through the education system, national youth organizations, and volunteer roles. (p. 309)

Omitted from this source of recommendations (Subcommittee on Aging of the Committee on Labor and Public Welfare and Special Committee on Aging, United States Senate, 1973) is a preamble to the report of the Employment and Retirement Section (no date) of the 1971 White House Conference on Aging that makes a general emphasis not to be neglected:

"Freedom, independence and the free exercise of individual initiative in planning and managing their own lives" was declared an objective for older Americans in the 1965 Older Americans Act. This includes freedom to choose in their later years between retiring on an adequate income or continuing in employment, full-time, or part-time, if they are able to do so. This free choice, however, is still denied to most older citizens. . . . (p. 1)

In all the areas discussed in this monograph, older persons are entitled to a broadened range of options and increased participation in decision-making, certainly in a society whose keystone is freedom of choice.

## SUMMARY

To maximize their effectiveness, counselors must become familiar with the social and legislative contexts affecting the lives of older persons. Programmatic trends indicating progress are outnumbered by unresolved issues regarding retirement, employment, and where people live and die. Numerous recommendations are offered toward resolution of critical issues and added recognition of the rights of older persons.

*Appendix 1*

# READING RELATED TO
# OLDER WOMEN

Andreas, C. *Sex and caste in America.* Englewood Cliffs, N. J.: Prentice-Hall, 1971.

Angel, J. L. *Matching college women to jobs.* New York: Simon & Schuster, 1970.

Astin, H. S., Suniewick, N., & Dweck, S. *Women: A bibliography on their education and careers.* Washington, D. C.: Human Service Press, 1971.

Baker, E. F. *Technology and woman's work.* New York: Columbia University Press, 1964.

Bardwick, J. M. *The psychology of women: A study of bio-cultural conflicts.* New York: Harper & Row, 1971.

Caine, L. *Widow.* New York: Morrow, 1974.

Champagne, M. G. *Facing life alone: What widows and divorcées should know.* Indianapolis: Bobbs-Merrill, 1964.

Davis, M. *Get the most out of your best years: The intelligent woman's guide.* New York: Dial Press, 1960.

DuBrin, A. J. *Survival in the sexist jungle.* Chatsworth, Calif.: Books for Better Living, 1974.

Epstein, C. F. *Woman's place: Options and limits in professional careers.* Berkeley: University of California Press, 1971.

Gross, I. H. (Ed.). *Potentialities of women in the middle years.* East Lansing: Michigan State University Press, 1956.

Huber, J. (Ed.). *Changing women in a changing society.* Chicago: University of Chicago Press, 1973.

Kanowitz, L. *Sex roles in law and society: Cases and materials.* Albuquerque: University of New Mexico Press, 1973.

Komarovsky, M. *Blue-collar marriage.* New York: Vintage Books, 1967.

Kreps, J. *Sex in the marketplace: American women at work.* Baltimore: Johns Hopkins Press, 1971.

Kutner, L. *The intelligent woman's guide to future security.* New York: Dodd Mead, 1970.

Langer, M. *Learning to live as a widow.* New York: Julian Messner, 1957.

Lembeck, R. *Job ideas for today's woman.* Englewood Cliffs, N. J.: Prentice-Hall, 1974.

Lewis, A., & Bobroff, E. *From kitchen to career.* Indianapolis: Bobbs-Merrill, 1965.

Lewis, E. C. *Developing women's potential.* Ames: Iowa State University Press, 1968.

Lifton, R. J. (Ed.). *The woman in America.* Boston: Beacon Press, 1965.

Maccoby, E. (Ed.). *The development of sex differences.* Stanford, Calif.: Stanford University Press, 1966.

Matthews, E. E., Feingold, S. N., Weary, B., Berry, J., & Tyler, L. E. *Counseling girls and women over the life span.* Washington, D. C.: National Vocational Guidance Association, 1972.

Morris, S. *Grief and how to live with it.* New York: Grosset & Dunlap, 1972.

National Manpower Council. *Womanpower.* New York: Columbia University Press, 1957.

O'Neill, B. P. *Careers for women after marriage and children.* New York: Macmillan, 1965.

Owens, L. H. *Toward more meaningful counseling with women.* Washington, D. C.: American Personnel and Guidance Association, 1970.

Parker, E. *The seven ages of woman.* Baltimore: Johns Hopkins Press, 1960.

Prentice, B. A. *The back-to-work handbook for housewives.* New York: Collier Books, 1971.

Ralston, M. *How to return to work in an office.* New York: Harper & Row, 1972.

Rapoport, R., & Rapoport, R. N. *Dual-career families.* Baltimore: Penguin Books, 1971.

Reeves, N. *Womankind: Beyond the stereotypes.* Chicago: Aldine-Atherton, 1971.

Rubin, I. *Sexual life after sixty.* New York: Basic Books, 1965.

Scobey, J., & McGrath, L. P. *Creative careers for women.* New York: Simon & Schuster, 1968.

Scott, A. F. *The American woman: Who was she?* Englewood Cliffs, N. J.: Prentice-Hall, 1971.

Simons, G. *What every woman doesn't know.* New York: Macmillan, 1964.

Smuts, R. W. *Women and work in America.* New York: Columbia University Press, 1959.

Splaver, S. *Nontraditional careers for women.* New York: Julian Messner, 1973.

Taves, I. *Women alone.* New York: Funk and Wagnalls, 1969.

Theodore, A. (Ed.). *The professional woman.* Cambridge, Mass.: Schenkman, 1971.

Women and counselors. (Special issue) *Personnel and Guidance Journal*, 1972, *51*, 81–160.

Women's Bureau, U. S. Department of Labor, Washington, D. C. 20210. Numerous pertinent publications, many free of charge.

*Appendix 2*

# PERIODICALS PERTINENT
# TO OLDER PERSONS

Adult Leadership
Aging
Aging and Human Development
American Journal of Sociology
American Sociological Review
Community Mental Health Journal
Counseling Psychologist
Dynamic Maturity
Geriatrics
Gerontologist
Harvest Years
Human Development
Impact
Industrial Gerontology
Journal of the American Geriatrics Society
Journal of Counseling Psychology
Journal of Gerontology
Journal of Health and Human Behavior
Journal of Human Relations
Journal of Marriage and the Family
Journal of Personality and Social Psychology
Journal of Rehabilitation
Journal of Social Issues
Journal of Thanatology
Mental Hygiene
Modern Maturity
Omega
Personnel and Guidance Journal
Perspective on Aging
Rehabilitation Counseling Bulletin
Rehabilitation Literature
Retired Officer
Retirement Life
Social and Rehabilitation Record
Social Casework
Social Forces
Social Work
Suicide
Vocational Guidance Quarterly

*Appendix 3*

# ORGANIZATIONS CONCERNED WITH OLDER PERSONS

American Association of Homes for the Aging
National Press Building
Washington, D. C. 20004

American Association of Retired Persons and National Retired Teachers Association
1909 K Street, N.W.
Washington, D. C. 20049

American Geriatrics Society
10 Columbus Circle
New York, N. Y. 10019

American Nursing Home Association
1025 Connecticut Avenue, N.W.
Washington, D. C. 20036

American Personnel and Guidance Association
1607 New Hampshire Avenue, N.W.
Washington, D. C. 20009

American Psychiatric Association
1700 18th Street, N.W.
Washington, D. C. 20009

American Psychological Association
1200 17th Street, N.W.
Washington, D. C. 20036

American Public Welfare Association
1313 East 60th Street
Chicago, Illinois 60637

American Women's Voluntary Services
125 East 65th Street
New York, N. Y. 10021

B'nai B'rith
1640 Rhode Island Avenue, N.W.
Washington, D. C. 20036

Board of Missions—United Methodist Church
475 Riverside Drive
New York, N. Y. 10027

Board of Social Ministry—Lutheran Church in America
231 Madison Avenue
New York, N. Y. 10016

Board of Women's Work—Presbyterian Church
341 Ponce de Leon Avenue, N.E.
Atlanta, Georgia 30308

Commission on Aging—Friends United Meeting
101 Quaker Hill Drive
Richmond, Indiana 47374

Conference of Health Services for the Aging—Catholic Hospital Association
1438 South Grand Boulevard
St. Louis, Missouri 63104

Council for Health and Welfare Services—United Church of Christ
287 Park Avenue South
New York, N. Y. 10010

Council of Jewish Federations and Welfare Funds
315 Park Avenue South
New York, N. Y. 10010

Council of the Southern Mountains
College Box 2307
Berea, Kentucky 40403

Council on Family Health
201 East 42nd Street
New York, N. Y. 10017

Episcopal Society for Ministry to
the Aging
c/o Bishop Penick Home
East Rhode Island Avenue Ext.
Southern Pines, North Carolina
28387

Family Service Association of
America
44 East 23rd Street
New York, N. Y. 10010

Farmers Union—Green Thumb
1012 14th Street N.W.
Washington, D. C. 20005

General Federation of Women's
Clubs
1734 N Street, N.W.
Washington, D. C. 20036

Gerontological Society
One Dupont Circle
Washington, D. C. 20036

Golden Ring Council of Senior
Citizens
22 West 38th Street
New York, N. Y. 10018

National Association for Mental
Health
1800 North Kent Street
Arlington, Virginia 22209

National Association of Jewish
Homes for the Aged
2525 Centerville Road
Dallas, Texas 75228

National Association of Retired
Federal Employees
1533 New Hampshire Avenue,
N.W.
Washington, D. C. 20009

National Association of Social
Workers
1425 H Street, N.W.
Washington, D. C. 20005

National Association of State
Units on Aging
1600 Sherman Street
Denver, Colorado 80218

National Center on the Black
Aged
1725 DeSales Street, N.W.
Washington, D. C. 20036

National Conference of Catholic
Charities
1346 Connecticut Avenue, N.W.
Washington, D. C. 20009

National Conference on Public
Employee Retirement Sys-
tems
88 East Broad Street
Columbus, Ohio 43215

National Conference on Social
Welfare
22 West Gay Street
Columbus, Ohio 43215

National Council for Homemaker
Services
1740 Broadway
New York, N. Y. 10019

National Council of Jewish Women
1625 Eye Street, N.W.
Washington, D. C. 20006

National Council of Jewish Women
1 West 47th Street
New York, N. Y. 10036

National Council of Senior Citizens
1627 K Street, N.W.
Washington, D. C. 20006

National Council on the Aging
1828 L Street, N.W.
Washington, D. C. 20036

National Council on Teacher Retirement
1390 Logan Street
Denver, Colorado 80203

National Easter Seal Society for Crippled Children and Adults
2023 West Ogden Avenue
Chicago, Illinois 60612

National Rehabilitation Association
1522 K Street, N.W.
Washington, D. C. 20005

National Society of the Volunteers of America
340 West 85th Street
New York, N. Y. 10024

National Therapeutic Recreation Society
1700 Pennsylvania Avenue, N.W.
Washington, D. C. 20006

Pilot Club International
244 College Street
P. O. Box 4844
Macon, Georgia 31208

Southern Baptist Association of Executives of Homes for the Aging
460 James Robertson Parkway
Nashville, Tennessee 37219

The Townsend Plan National Lobby
5500 Quincy Street
Hyattsville, Maryland 20784

United Health Foundations
150 Fifth Avenue
New York, N. Y. 10017

# REFERENCES

American Association of Retired Persons/National Retired Teachers Association. *1974 legislative objectives and 1974–75 sta'e guidelines*. Washington, D. C.: Author, 1974.

Arnold, S., Brock, J., Ledford, L., & Richards, H. *Ready or not: A study manual for retirement*. New York: Manpower Education Institute, 1974.

Arthur, J. K. *Retire to action: A guide to voluntary service*. Nashville: Abingdon Press, 1969.

Batchelor, I. R. C. Suicide in old age. In E. S. Shneidman & N. L. Farberow (Eds.), *Clues to suicide*. New York: McGraw-Hill, 1957. Pp. 143–151.

Belbin, R. M. *The discovery method: An effective technique for training older workers*. Paris: Organisation for Economic Cooperation and Development, 1968.

Belbin, R. M. The discovery method in training older workers. In. H. L. Sheppard (Ed.), *Toward an industrial gerontology*. Cambridge, Mass.: Schenkman Publishing Company, 1970. Pp. 56–60.

Botwinick, J. *Aging and behavior*. New York: Springer, 1973.

Bowers, M. K., Jackson, E. N., Knight, J. A., & LeShan, L. *Counseling the dying*. New York: Thomas Nelson & Sons, 1964.

Brochard, J. *School subjects and jobs*. Chicago: Science Research Associates, 1971.

Brotman, H. B. *Facts and figures on older Americans: An overview*. Washington, D. C.: Administration on Aging, 1971.

Butler, R. N., & Lewis, M. I. *Aging and mental health: Positive psychosocial approaches*. St. Louis: C. V. Mosby, 1973.

Cantor, J. M. The search for the suicidal personality. In K. Wolff (Ed.), *Patterns of self-destruction: Depression and suicide.* Springfield, Ill.: Charles C Thomas, 1970. Pp. 56–66.

Carey, R. G. Emotional adjustment in terminal patients: A quantitative approach. *Journal of Counseling Psychology,* 1974, *21,* 433–439.

Carp, F. M. (Ed.). *The retirement process.* Bethesda, Md.: National Institutes of Health, 1968.

Close, K. *Getting ready to retire.* New York: Public Affairs Pamphlets, 1972.

Collings, K. J. *The second time around: Finding a civilian career in midlife.* Cranston, R. I.: Carroll Press, 1971.

Crane, D. Dying and its dilemmas as a field of research. In O. G. Brim, Jr., H. E. Freeman, S. Levine, & N. A. Scotch (Eds.), *The dying patient.* New York: Russell Sage Foundation, 1970. Pp. 303–325.

Dailey, C. A. *Assessment of lives.* San Francisco: Jossey-Bass, 1971.

Doyle, N. *The dying person and the family.* New York: Public Affairs Committee, 1972.

Draper, J. E., Lundgren, E. F., & Strother, G. B. *Work attitudes and retirement adjustments.* Madison: University of Wisconsin, Bureau of Business Research and Service, 1967.

Eisdorfer, C., & Lawton, M. P. (Eds.) *The psychology of adult development and aging.* Washington, D. C.: American Psychological Association, 1973.

Employment and Retirement Section, 1971 White House Conference on Aging. *Section recommendations.* Superintendent of Documents, U. S. Government Printing Office, Washington, D. C. 20402. No date.

Erikson, E. H. *Childhood and society.* (2nd ed.). New York: W. W. Norton, 1963.

Farberow, N. L., & Shneidman, E. S. (Eds.). *The cry for help.* New York: McGraw-Hill, 1961.

Feder, S. L. Attitudes of patients with advanced malignancy. In Group for the Advancement of Psychiatry, *Death and dying: Attitudes of patient and doctor.* New York: Author, 1965. Pp. 614–622.

Feifel, H. Some aspects of the meaning of death. In E. S. Shneidman & N. L. Farberow (Eds.), *Clues to suicide.* New York: McGraw-Hill, 1957. Pp. 50–57.

Feifel, H. The function of attitudes toward death. In Group for the Advancement of Psychiatry, *Death and dying: Attitudes of patient and doctor*. New York: Author, 1965. Pp. 632–641.

Feifel, H. The meaning of dying in American society. In R. H. David (Ed.), *Dealing with death*. Los Angeles: Andrus Gerontology Center, University of Southern California, 1973. Pp. 1–8.

Frankl, V. *Man's search for meaning: An introduction to logotherapy*. New York: Washington Square Press, 1963.

Gallup, G., Jr. Are we living up to the promise of America? *Vocational Guidance Quarterly*, 1974, *23*, 105–111.

Ginzberg, E. Toward a theory of occupational choice: A restatement. *Vocational Guidance Quarterly*, 1972, *20*, 169–176.

Goodman, S. E. *National directory of adult and continuing education*. Piscataway, N. J.: Education and Training Associates, 1968.

Grace, H. A. Industrial gerontology: Behavioral science perspectives on work and aging. In *Industrial gerontology: Curriculum materials*. New York: National Council on the Aging, 1968. Pp. 1–84.

Green, R. F. Age, intelligence, and learning. *Industrial Gerontology*, 1972, *12*, 29–41.

Griew, S. *Job redesign*. Paris: Organisation for Economic Cooperation and Development, 1964.

Grinker, R. R., Sr. The psychodynamics of suicide and attempted suicide. In L. Yochelson (Ed.), *Symposium on suicide*. Washington, D. C.: George Washington University, 1967, Pp. 60–70.

Grollman, E. A. *Suicide: Prevention, intervention, postvention*. Boston: Beacon Press, 1971.

Grollman, E. A. (Ed.). *Concerning death: A practical guide for the living*. Boston: Beacon Press, 1974.

Group for the Advancement of Psychiatry. *The right to die*. New York: Aronson, 1974.

Hickey, T., & Szabo, K. Grief intervention and the helping professional. In T. Hickey (Ed.), *Grief: Its recognition and resolution*. University Park: Pennsylvania State University, 1973. Pp. 1–15.

Hiestand, D. L. *Changing careers after thirty-five: New horizons through professional and graduate study*. New York: Columbia University Press, 1971.

Hunter, W. W. *Preparation for retirement*. Ann Arbor: University of Michigan, 1968.

Jourard, S. M. Suicide: an invitation to die. In M. H. Browning and E. P. Lewis (Eds.), *The dying patient: A nursing perspective*. New York: American Journal of Nursing Company, 1972. Pp. 49–55.

Kastenbaum, R. Death and bereavement in later life. In A. H. Kutscher (Ed.), *Death and bereavement*. Springfield, Ill.: Charles C Thomas, 1969 (a) Pp. 28–54.

Kastenbaum, R. Psychological death. In L. Pearson (Ed.), *Death and dying: Current issues in the treatment of the dying person*. Cleveland: Case Western Reserve University Press, 1969. (b) Pp. 1–27.

Kastenbaum, R., & Aisenberg, R. *The psychology of death*. New York: Springer, 1972.

Kimmel, D. C. *Adulthood and aging: An interdisciplinary, developmental view*. New York: Wiley, 1974.

Koller, M. R. *Social gerontology*. New York: Random House, 1968.

Koyl, L. F. A technique for measuring functional criteria in placement and retirement practices. In H. L. Sheppard (Ed.), *Toward an industrial gerontology*. Cambridge, Mass.: Schenkman Publishing Company, 1970. Pp. 140–156.

Koyl, L. F., Hackney, M., & Holloway, R. D. *Employing the older worker: Matching the employee to the job*. (2nd ed.). Washington, D. C.: National Council on the Aging, 1974.

Krupp, G. R., & Kligfeld, B. The bereavement reaction: A cross-cultural evaluation. In R. B. Reeves, Jr., R. E. Neale, & A. H. Kutscher, *Pastoral care of the dying and the bereaved*. New York: Health Sciences Publishing Corp., 1973. Pp. 125–149.

Kübler-Ross, E. *On death and dying*. New York: Macmillan, 1969.

Kutscher, A. H. (Ed.). *Death and bereavement*. Springfield, Ill.: Charles C Thomas, 1969.

Laas, W. *Helpful hints on managing your money for retirement*. New York: Popular Library, 1970.

Lasagna, L. The prognosis of death. In O. G. Brim, Jr., H. E. Freeman, S. Levine, and N. A. Scotch (Eds.), *The dying patient*. New York: Russell Sage Foundation, 1970. Pp. 67–82.

Lawton, G., & Stewart, M. S. *When you grow older*. New York: Public Affairs Pamphlets, 1968.

LeShan, L. Psychotherapy and the dying patient. In L. Pearson (Ed.), *Death and dying: Current issues in the treatment of the dying person*. Cleveland: Case Western Reserve University Press, 1969. Pp. 28–48.

Leshner, S. S., & Snyderman, G. S. Evaluating personal characteristics from a client's work history. *Personnel and Guidance Journal*, 1963, *42*, 56–59.

Maddox, G. L. Retirement as a social event in the United States. In B. L. Neugarten (Ed.), *Middle age and aging*. Chicago: University of Chicago Press, 1968. Pp. 357–365.

Malnig, L. R., & Morrow, S. L. *What can I do with a major in. . . ?* Jersey City: Saint Peter's College Press, 1975.

Marbach, G. *Job redesign for older workers*. Paris: Organisation for

Economic Cooperation and Development, 1968.

McGarraghy, J. J. The external degree program: One avenue to a second career. *Industrial Gerontology*, Spring 1973 (No. 17), 61–66.

National Council on the Aging. *Recommendations for action in the 70's*. Washington, D. C.: The Council, no date.

Neale, R. E. *The art of dying*. New York: Harper & Row, 1973.

Overs, R. P., O'Connor, E., & DeMarco, B. *Avocational activities for the handicapped: A handbook for avocational counseling*. Springfield, Ill.: Charles C Thomas, 1974.

Palmore, E., & Jeffers, F. C. (Eds.). *Prediction of life span*. Lexington, Mass.: D. C. Heath, 1971.

Paul, N. Psychiatry: Its role in the resolution of grief. In A. H. Kutscher (Ed.), *Death and bereavement*. Springfield, Ill.: Charles C Thomas, 1969. Pp. 174–195.

Pollak, O. *Positive experiences in retirement*. Homewood, Ill.: Richard D. Irwin, 1957.

Puner, M. *To the good long life: What we know about growing old*. New York: Universe Books, 1974.

Quirk, D. A. *Campaign 1974: Toward a responsive social policy for the elderly*. Washington, D. C.: National Council on the Aging, 1974.

Reik, T. *Listening with the third ear*. New York: Farrar Strauss, 1949.

Riley, M. W., & Foner, A. *Aging and society* (Vol. I). New York: Russell Sage Foundation, 1968.

Rome, H. P. Motives for suicide. In K. Wolff (Ed.), *Patterns of self-destruction: Depression and suicide*. Springfield, Ill.: Charles C Thomas, 1970. Pp. 43–55.

Rose, C. L., & Bell, B. *Predicting longevity*. Lexington, Mass.: D. C. Heath, 1971.

Saunders, C. The moment of truth: Care of the dying person. In L. Pearson (Ed.), *Death and dying: Current issues in the treatment of the dying person*. Cleveland: Case Western Reserve University Press, 1969. Pp. 49–78.

Schlossberg, N. K., Vontress, C. E., & Sinick, D. Dynamics of client-counselor differences. *Vocational Guidance Quarterly*, 1974, *23*, 29–33.

Sheppard, H. L., Ullmann, C. A., Cooperman, I. G., & Samler, J. Second careers as a way of life: A symposium. *Vocational Guidance Quarterly*, 1971, *20*, 89–118.

Shneidman, E. S. *Deaths of man*. New York: Quadrangle/The New York Times Book Co., 1973.

Sinick, D. *Occupational information and guidance*. Boston: Houghton Mifflin, 1970.

Smith, P. C., Kendall, L. M., & Hulin, C. L. *The measurement of satisfaction in work and retirement*. Chicago: Rand McNally, 1969.

Social Security Administration, U. S. Department of Health, Education, and Welfare. *Design for dignity: Supplemental security for the aged, blind, and disabled*. Washington, D. C.: The Administration, 1973.

Special Committee on Aging, United States Senate. *Developments in aging: 1973 and January-March 1974*. (93rd Congress, 2nd Session, Report No. 93–846.) Washington, D. C.: U. S. Government Printing Office, 1974.

Steinberg, J. L. *Guide to careers through college majors*. San Diego: Robert R. Knapp, 1964.

Stetson, D. *Starting over*. New York: Macmillan, 1971.

Subcommittee on Aging of the Committee on Labor and Public Welfare and Special Committee on Aging, United States Senate. *Post-White House Conference on Aging Reports, 1973*. Washington, D. C.: Superintendent of Documents, U. S. Government Printing Office, 1973.

Sudnow, D. *Passing on*. Englewood Cliffs, N. J.: Prentice-Hall, 1967.

Sullivan, H. S. *The interpersonal theory of psychiatry*. New York: Norton, 1953.

Super, D. E. *Avocational interest patterns: A study in the psychology of avocations*. Stanford, California: Stanford University Press, 1940.

Thomson, F. C. (Ed.) *The New York Times guide to continuing education in America*. New York: Quadrangle Books, 1972.

Tiven, M. B. *Older Americans: Special handling required*. Washington, D. C.: National Council on the Aging, 1971.

Troll, L., & Schlossberg, N. How "age biased" are college counselors? *Industrial Gerontology*, 1971, *10*, 14–21.

U. S. Civil Service Commission. *Retirement planning programs*. Washington, D. C.: Author, 1968.

U. S. Department of Defense. *Target—tomorrow: Second career planning for military retirees*. Washington, D. C.: Superintendent of Documents, U. S. Government Printing Office, 1970.

U. S. Department of Labor. *Counseling and placement services for older workers*. Washington, D. C.: Superintendent of Documents, U. S. Government Printing Office, 1956.

U. S. Department of Labor. *Dictionary of occupational titles* (3rd ed.). Volume I, *Definitions of titles*. Volume II, *Occupational classification*. Washington, D. C.: Superintendent of Documents, U. S.

Government Printing Office, 1965.

U. S. Department of Labor. *A supplement to the dictionary of occupational titles* (3rd ed.). Washington, D. C.: Superintendent of Documents, U. S. Government Printing Office, 1966.

U. S. Department of Labor. *College courses and beginning jobs.* Washington, D. C.: Superintendent of Documents, U. S. Government Printing Office, 1967. (a)

U. S. Department of Labor. *Job redesign for older workers: Ten case studies.* Washington, D. C.: Superintendent of Documents, U. S. Government Printing Office, 1967.(b)

U. S. Department of Labor. *Education and jobs.* Washington, D. C.: Superintendent of Documents, U. S. Government Printing Office, 1968.(a)

U. S. Department of Labor. *Supplement 2 to the dictionary of occupational titles* (3rd ed.). Washington, D. C.: Superintendent of Documents, U. S. Government Printing Office, 1968.(b)

U. S. Department of Labor. *Americans volunteer.* Washington, D. C.: Superintendent of Documents, U. S. Government Printing Office, 1969.

U. S. Department of Labor. *U. S. manpower in the 1970's: Opportunity and challenge.* Washington, D. C.: Superintendent of Documents, U. S. Government Printing Office, 1970.

U. S. Department of Labor. *Back to work after retirement.* Washington, D. C.: Superintendent of Documents, U. S. Government Printing Office, 1971.(a)

U. S. Department of Labor. *Continuing education programs and services for women.* Washington, D. C.: Superintendent of Documents, U. S. Government Printing Office, 1971.(b)

U. S. Department of Labor. *Get credit for what you know.* Washington, D. C.: Author, 1971.(c)

U. S. Department of Labor. *The employment problems of older workers.* Washington, D. C.: Superintendent of Documents, U. S. Government Printing Office, 1971.(d)

U. S. Department of Labor. Series: Biology and your career, English and your career, Foreign languages and your career, Math and your career, Science and your career, Social science and your career. Washington, D. C.: Author, even years.

Wahl, C. W. Psychological treatment of the dying patient. In J. Q. Benoliel, H. Feifel, E. S. Shneidman, C. W. Wahl, & E. H. Waechter, *Dealing with death.* Los Angeles: Ethel Percy Andrus Gerontology Center, University of Southern California, 1973. Pp. 9–23.

Weisman, A. D. *On dying and denying: A psychiatric study of terminality.* New York: Behavioral Publications, 1972.

Whitfield, E. A., & Hoover, R. *Guide to careers through vocational training.* San Diego: Robert R. Knapp, 1968.

Whitney, D. R. Predicting from expressed vocational choice: A review. *Personnel and Guidance Journal,* 1969, *48,* 279–286.